Table of Content.  Pages

WINNING THE HEART OF GOD

KNOWING GOD'S SECRETS - LIKE KING DAVID.

Author- Akua Osei-Bonsu

Akua Osei-Bonsu received her associate's degree in financial banking in Ghana. As a member of the Ghana Institutes of Banker's in 1988, she initially was focused on making a successful Banking career in Europe.

But God called her into the Ministry as an Evangelist and a Prophetess after a radical transformation in 1993. She went through a near death experience as she tried to run away from the calling of God!

But graciously, God brought her back from the grips of death even though doctors could not identify the cause of her ailment and declared she had no hope! Not only did she live, but she lives with a greater passion for life and for people as a result of the death experience and graphic scenes she saw of hell.

Akua studied at the Amsterdam Bible Academy for 2 years which was affiliated with Irving University in Texas and earned a diploma in Practical Ministry. She was ordained as a Minister by Morris Cerullo Ministry after completing a correspondence School of Ministry. She also had two years Prophetic Training at the Christian International FL, U.S.A.

She continued her Biblical training by studying Practical Ministry at the Wagner Leadership Institute in California and pursued her doctorate in Practical Ministry and Theology at the Everlasting Chip University in California.

She is in the process of coordinating networks of intercessors globally, is a Bible Teacher and also hosts TV Programs at The Cross TV (www.thecrosstv.com) and also at OCN Broadcasting (www.ocn.com).

Acknowledgement

I want to thank God for the thoughts He gave me for this book I am grateful for the Holy Spirit who guided me even when things seemed impossible. I thank Mr. Mike V. Howell, Pastor Ernest Witmer of the L.A. ROAD Ministries who helped me with the editing, Dr. Bruno Caporrimo founder of Everlasting CHIP University/Ministries, who encouraged me on several occasions. Thanks to my family for their support especially my son Benny and nieces who challenged me to study hard.

Special thanks to all the people who have supported me financially. Lastly, I thank all my Pastors at the HRock Church especially Pastor Che Ahn for the legacy.

This book is dedicated to people who are seeking for more of God especially my spiritual father Pastor Gordon Lee (former Pastor of Full Gospel Trinity Church in Los Angeles). And people who do not have a revelation of God: people who want to know God's secrets!

God is no respecter of persons. God loves us all. He demonstrates this through the death and resurrection of His Son. There's nothing difficult on our part to show that we love Him.

However; the more we draw closer to him the more we can win his heart. He Reveals His Secrets to those who fear Him.

Endorsements

What does it take to know God intimately? Throughout the centuries, certain individuals seem to find the way closer to God's heart than others. Just what is it that makes God call someone "after His own heart"?

The new book "Winning the Heart of God" presents a Scriptural portrait of King David's life and unpacks practical lessons that will help mold your heart to be more like God's. As a member of HRock Church, Akua Osei-Bonsu articulates biblical truths in these pages, providing strength and encouragement for your relationship with God. I recommend this book for anyone desiring a closer walk with the Lord!

Dr. Ché Ahn
Founding Pastor, HROCK Church, Pasadena, CA
President, Harvest International Ministry
International Chancellor, Wagner Leadership Institute

I am delighted to share that Dr Akua Osei-Bonsu's inspirational book is very balanced. It is needed today for all ages from five to ninety. She briefly covered every point from to know God and to know His Ways and all the principles for our daily life. It gives inspiration, insight of the Word of God to His children to apply to our daily life. So if you are hungry to know the Lord in an intimate way and walk into His relationship, then this inspirational book is written specially for you. Get a copy, read it all and get it all. Press it on!
Truly, The Servant of God.

Dr. Bruno Caporrimo,
Founder - Joseph Global Institute, Everlasting CHIP Ministry/ University.

I was blessed by Akua's testimony from the very first time I met her: Her story of redemption in the midst of her own personal struggle, her everyday burden for lost souls, and especially by her passion in prayer. The thunderous reverberations of heaven's door echo back to earth every time she pounds them in prayer! She will often spend 8-10 hours at a time, locked in the privacy of her bedroom, passionately interceding for others. She is also not ashamed to cry out to the Lord loudly in public as well! Truly she knows how to gain the heart of God!

Everything Akua writes in this book she has lived. She is indeed a delightful daughter of God and relates to Him as her own loving Father. I've seen her rebuffed and belittled by people... even those she should have been able to count on, yet she forgives and moves on.

"If I don't forgive, she says, I can't pray. And I must pray!"

And so she forgives! Again winning the heart of God.

Hardly a day goes by that she has not led someone else to a born-again experience in Christ. Just yesterday as she was washing her car and handing out Gospel leaflets to others around her, someone asked her,

"Is this about Jesus?"

"Yes," she said.

"Can you tell me how I can make Him a part of my life," he inquired.

"Of course I will tell you," she responded, and promptly led him to place his faith in Jesus Christ for salvation.

Now why did he ask her, you might ask? The answer is simple: Because she pursues the Lord herself with a determination that is contagious to others. Whether it's random fellows at car washes, Chinese women merchants on Main Street, or the homeless on skid row, Akua is constantly caring for people and speaking prophetically into their lives. Please read this book and you will know not only how to win the heart of God, but how to make His heart your heart too.

Pastor Ernest Witmer, L.A. ROAD (Los Angeles' Real-life Opportunities And Discipleship)

Winning the Heart of God

Knowing God's Secrets - like King David

Introduction: We all have secrets we will never reveal to people that cannot be trusted. In the same way God has many secrets that He wants to reveal to you, provided that you can be trusted.

Do you want to know some of these hidden treasures? We are going to journey through this book to capture some of God's secret revelations with individuals he could trust.

God can turn the heart of a King in the direction He wants and once upon a time there was a King who won God's heart. Let's take a journey through the life of this King – King David and some other famous individuals who lived to know the secrets of God. Is it easy to know God's secrets?

Well, I believe you will find the answer by the time you finish reading this book. As a child you may have tried to get your parents attention in one of two ways

Maybe your reaction was positive and you tried to study harder, keep your room clean or something else. Or maybe your reaction was negative, like crying or pouting in the grocery store line.

There are many ways you could choose to gain your parents attention. It ultimately depends on your mode of "determination." Whatever we feel is right will determine our heart's direction.

God loves us unconditionally. We do not have to please God when it is about our salvation, because he loved us even while we were sinners. However; the revelation of God for us will certainly depend on our intimacy with Him.

The more we seek Him the more we find and know His secrets. The more we know His secrets the more we love Him. If you want to have that relationship or know more about God there is a prayer after the last chapter; please pray that prayer.

King David was the second King of Israel and the most famous and influential King in the history of Israel. The Jews still believe that King David was the most accomplished King they have ever had. Besides ruling over Israel, he was a shepherd, a musician, a worshipper and a mighty warrior.

All his skills were a blessing from God and he loved and honored God. It is recorded that of the one hundred and fifty songs of Psalms, he is responsible for about seventy-eight of them. The book of Psalms is credited to him because he compiled and established them in a form of worship and also instituted the practice of worship with inspirational songs.

King David was to build the first Temple in Jerusalem. The temple was very precious to the Jews. It was his desire to build temple but God forbade him because his hands were covered with the blood of people he had killed in wars and battles.

He also killed Uriah, one of his army captains who he murdered to cover-up his sins after committing adultery with his wife Bathsheba.

To this day, the Jews cherish the temple because they believe in Congregational worship. The Torah (the first five books of the Old Testament) would be read to both young and old in the Temple.

God instructed that his son, Solomon should therefore build it. However, the whole plan (architecture, worship sets and the finance to build) were mainly provided and organized by King David.

One of the most popular stories of King David's life is about his battle with Goliath. It has been told in many ways and is probably one of the most common Bible stories besides the Nativity of Christ.

A lot of children hear the story in Sunday school class or watch the David and Goliath cartoons on Television or videos. The story tells us how David slew the Philistine giant named Goliath who had taunted and defiled the Israelites' God for forty days.

King David left these remarkable legacies for all of us to admire, but he was an ordinary man who had been used by God to do great exploits and extraordinary.

David was just a little shepherd boy but it did not disqualify him from being king, for he was God's anointed and appointed ruler over the Israelites.

God made a remarkable statement in scripture regarding David that was similar to what He said about Abraham and his Son Jesus.

"I have found David, a man after My own heart and he will do whatever I tell him." Acts 13:22

Despite King David's great successes and achievements, he had flaws like any other man. He committed adultery with Bathsheba and killed her husband, Uriah. This brought a lot of chaos in his household. He failed to correct his son, Ammon, who raped his half-sister Tamar. This led to further family turmoil as Tamar's brother Absalom dethroned his father David.

King David was very weak at disciplining his children. Perhaps his conscience condemned him from correcting his sons since he himself had sinned even more.

Perhaps he just did not know how to nurture his children. After all he was a warrior and spent most of his time on the battlefield.

Ultimately, King David's sin opened a door for the devil to get a stronghold in his life.

Winning the Heart of God is discovering the deeper experience of the secrets and ways of God that would give David more desire (appetite) and understanding of who God was and is.

You can change every area of your life; spiritually, financially, emotionally, relationally, etc. as you read this book and follow King David's pursuit of God.

I pray that the lessons in this book will cause you to do great exploits as you learn how to win the heart of God

God bless you as you read it.

Therefore whoever humbles himself as this little child is the greatest in the Kingdom of Heaven (Matthew 18:4).

Chapter 1

Humble Spirit - The State of Vulnerability.

The Scriptures tell us that God can turn the heart of a King in whichever way He wants. "The king's heart is like a stream of water directed by the LORD; he guides it wherever he pleases" (Proverbs 21:1).

Irrespective of our status, God has the power to change the heart, mind and thoughts of a person because He is Omnipotent.
However, God has also given you your own free will. He did not create you as a machine or robot.

Because man has his freewill, it is easy for man to be tempted and sin of pride. It does not matter if you are in a high or low position in society; pride can be deceptively domineering! This is a concern as we begin our journey of understanding the humble in spirit. It is a journey that is required to enter the heart of God!

The spirit of pride is more prevalent and less detectable in our own minds than we are willing to admit!

Therefore we can all be prideful in one way or another. God knows the heart of man yet His eyes are searching to and fro throughout the earth searching for people who really possess a humble heart!

Why? Because the humble in heart will possess the strength of God! King David had a humble and teachable spirit. The Greek word for "humble" is, "shapel" or "tapeinos." Primarily it means to be low, become low, low-lying or be submissive. In the original ancient Hebrew language, it meant to be afflicted, meek, or to bow down.

However, humbleness is certainly not weakness, but it is the state of being vulnerable (open to a better way) and transparent (honest heart) before God and man.

It is one of the keys to a successful (satisfied) spiritual life in the Kingdom of God. It is seeing yourself in the strength and confidence that you are pursuing God's heart. It is when you want the knowledge of God for who He is.

King David knew and admitted that his achievements and successes in all his life, the wars and battles he had engaged in, were all a result of his trust in God (2 Samuel 22:31-37). He learned even from his childhood that if he would commit his ways to the Lord, God would guide his path (Psalm 37).
King David knew how his heart could be deceptively proud, so he was always careful to give God the glory (credit) in every victory and success.

It is very easy for us to take the glory that belongs to God, especially when we are skilled, talented or gifted. Pride is inevitable whenever we think our own strength or ability makes us successful.

A humble spirit draws us closer to the Lord while pride easily builds walls of separation between us and God. King David knew the secret to having a close relationship with God was by loving and obeying Him. He knew God's language; the language of love!

The "love language" is how to express heartfelt commitment to your spouse, and likewise scripture describes the church as the bride of Christ. God also displays this similar relationship to the Jews.

David also knew God's Word and really loved Him. We cannot love God without loving His Word, because He and His Word are one (John 1:1).

The Lord said we cannot call Him Lord and not be willing to do His will (Luke 6:46). King David's heart was to please God in all that he did. H desperately needed the Divine presence (fellowship and direction) of God and as a result he knew a humble heart was a requirement of that journey.

Humbleness versus Pride.

Pride is therefore the opposite of humbleness. The word "opposes" in Greek is "anthistemi" which means to set against or to withstand. God therefore sets a limit that the proud will not exceed before consequences eventually begin to surface.

This is why we need God's grace or unmerited favor, a gift that we cannot purchase. However, we earn it freely from God, through our faith in Christ. Grace has a reflux mechanism that opposes pride.

Our Lord humbled Himself and God exalted Him (Philippians 2:5-9). On the other side of the coin, we see how pride cost Lucifer to lose his position in heaven. He was cast down from Heaven with a third of the angels just because he wanted to be worshipped like God (Revelation 12:4-7).

David's humbleness is reflected in the recordings of his prayers in the book of Psalms. He did not take the mercies of God for granted and it is an example to us all. David was thankful and for both the simple and great things God did for him. God's grace is free but we have to be careful how we handle it. We cannot abuse it because there are consequences for that.

For example, in Psalm 25 David asked God to show him His ways and teach him His path because he was teachable. I believe he asked God because he wanted to please God in all that he did.

If we are teachable, we are willing to accept correction and go in the right direction. This is the only way to maximizing our potential and fulfilling our dreams! Therefore, you and I have to ask God whatever we need in order to fulfill His purpose in our life! Because we were created for a purpose!

David uses the word meek in most of the Psalms which means humble or submissive. "I say to the LORD, "You are my Lord; apart from you I have no good thing" (Psalm 16:2, Psalm 37:11). He also spoke about the humble inheriting the earth in one of his songs (Psalm 34: 6). "This poor man cried, the Lord heard him and saved him out of all his troubles."

Our Lord confirmed in the beatitudes that the Kingdom belongs to the humble in spirit. "Blessed are the poor in spirit for theirs is the kingdom of God" (Matthew 5:3). The poor in spirit are those who know they are spiritually weak and that they need the strength of God.

David knew that he was poor in spirit and therefore needed God. How often do we see ourselves as poor in the spirit? Do you cry out to God when you are in dire need of help and wait on Him when all things around you seem impossible or do you look for an alternate solution, a "plan B?"

16

The Scriptures also describe King David as having a contrite heart. A contrite heart is a humble heart. It makes the heart easily convicted and open to repentance and God loves such people. He will not despise them (Psalm 51:17). "The sacrifices of God *are* a broken spirit; a broken and a contrite heart—These, O God, You will not despise."

He had the ability to be convicted and to repent when he had sinned. Even in adultery and murder! It happened when he committed adultery with Uriah's wife. Uriah was one of his best soldiers. David tried to cover up his sins when he had an adulterous affair. He first tried to make the child looked like it was Uriah's and not his own.

Because Uriah had been on the battlefield, he devised a plan to bring him home to his wife. However, Uriah did not want to go home to be with his wife, because he thought it was a season of war so why should he go and sleep comfortably with his wife while Israel was in danger?

Instead of going home Uriah decided to stay at King David's Palace with the servants. David tried to persuade him to go home so he could have the opportunity to lay with his wife and believe the child was conceived by him. When Uriah would not budge, David sent him back to the battlefield and commanded that he should be sent to the front lines where his life would be in danger.

David killed Uriah
After King David had Uriah purposely killed on the battlefield, he married his wife Bathsheba. This made God unhappy and against

what he did. He sent the Prophet Nathan to King David to expose his sin and bring judgment upon him and his household. Fortunately, David repented and from the story, Psalms 32 and 51 were written.

The genealogy of our Lord Jesus in the gospel of Matthew indicates that Bathsheba, Solomon's mother, was Uriah's wife. But of course, Solomon was the son of David and Bathsheba.

King David committed this very sin at a time that Kings went to war. This means David should have been at war during that period, but he decided to stay home and delegate. Though the scriptures didn't state why he delegated instead of being present. However it is human nature when God brings us out of trials we try to take a long rest and get stuck in our comfort zones.

Unfortunately, he fell into temptation and sinned. We can relate to David in many ways. Doing the right thing at the right time is imperative for each of us. David had been purpose-driven until he lost focus and sinned against God.

However, the Scriptures say that the righteous fall seven times but gets up each time. We must also stand up when we fall. It is not a time to accuse others, get excuses from the devil, or to condemn ourselves.

Admitting our sins, like David, is very important and is the best way to get closer to God. He ran to the light instead of running to the darkness. He accepted full responsibility for his sins. He did not shift the blame to Bathsheba like Adam did to Eve when He had sinned.

We have all been guilty of handling our sins like Adam and Eve when they sinned against God. Adam blamed Eve and she in turn blamed the serpent or the devil.

The phrase commonly used is "The devil made me do it" (Genesis 3:11-13). God is always about the business of restoration. Thus when we read the scriptures from Genesis to Revelation, we see God promising restoration to mankind right from the Garden of Eden to through the Israelites coming from Egypt as slaves and to the end of time. Jesus came to restore us back to God the Father through His death and resurrection. He is also coming to restore all things and to rule and reign over a restored world.

Humbleness in Leadership

David's humility helped him to lead by example. His humble leadership attracted mighty warriors who were with him from the time he killed Goliath till he became a King over Israel (He ruled approximately 14 years. He killed Goliath when he was about 16 years old and he was King over Israel at the age of 30) 2 Samuel 5:4. Those mighty men had no fear for their life and were ready to die for David when the need arose.

Talking about David 's humility, the scripture records how the Lord also humbled himself even unto death on the cross (Philippians 2:8). Jesus humbled Himself, from royalty to servant hood. Can you imagine going to the palace and seeing the King dressed like one of his servants and serving publicly? The Lord also demonstrated humility toward His disciples by washing their feet and He expects that same humbleness for us between one another.

19

Life on earth could have been more wonderfully lived by all people and, especially the children of God if we understood this principle! It would have been easier to share Jesus with the world. The Lord expects us to lead and live by his example and face the challenges to also "wash feet" in humility (John 13:1-17).

Slaves washed their master's hands and feet in those days and Israel's main transportation system was walking, riding donkeys, camels and boats. The roads were very dusty and when you entered a house the first duty was to wash your hands and feet. The literal washing of hands and feet do not make us clean in our heart, but is an outward example of humility so we can know the importance of serving one another, even the least among us.

In the Lord's day Jews were critical about Jesus' disciples when they saw two of them eating with "unclean" hands. Washing before eating is a Jewish ritual and "The Pharisees and some of the teachers of the law who had come from Jerusalem gathered around Jesus and saw some of his disciples eating food with hands that were defiled, that is, unwashed.

The Pharisees and all the Jews do not eat unless they give their hands a ceremonial washing, holding to the tradition of the elders. When they come from the marketplace they do not eat unless they wash. And they observe many other traditions, such as the washing of cups, pitchers and kettles" (Mark 7:1-4). Our Lord responded by stating that it is not what goes into the body that defiles it, but what comes out of it.

King David was anointed as a King over Israel by the Prophet Samuel when he was just a teenager. However, he did not rule till he was thirty years old (1 Samuel 16: 13, 2 Samuel 5:4). He humbled himself and served King Saul until his appointed time.

But he lived from cave to cave as the jealous King Saul sought to kill him. David was popular among the Israelites and he was the Old Testament example of our Lord Jesus in terms of humility.

How often have we seen deacons or elders of the church trying to teach Pastors how to pastor and lead their churches? We might even be guilty ourselves. We may do it because of selfish ambition, immaturity or other reasons but God does not take these acts lightly. He anoints, appoints and speaks to His leaders differently than He does to the body. Just as Moses, Abraham and Joseph; it took a humble spirit to gain favor in the sight of God because He always gives grace to the humble.

Being humble is hard to achieve, but it is a worthy accomplishment. The Scripture tells us that Moses was the most humble person on the face of this planet. "Now the man Moses was very meek (gentle, kind and humble) or above all the men on the face of the earth (Numbers 12:3 Amp). There's no doubt God spoke with him face to face because he received God's favor. Moses told God to show him His glory if he had found favor with Him and certainly God did (Exodus 33:13-18).

Our Lord Jesus came to earth to show us the way to the Father and to be a model for us. He taught us humility and to worship God in spirit and in truth.

One time the disciples were arguing who was the greatest among them. Surprisingly, Jesus called a child to them and told them that unless they humble themselves like a child, they cannot enter the Kingdom of God. "Whoever will humble himself therefore and become like this little child (trusting, lowly, loving, forgiving) is greatest in the Kingdom of Heaven" (Matthew 18:4 Amp). If you are a parent you know how your kids can act, and even if you are not you have been a child before. Children easily forget the hurt or pain they have experienced. They can play, fight and cry over a toy or something simple. But the next minute they can be playing together and have no record of the wrong.

Adults tend to remember the past when dealing with others. As adults, sometimes we find it really hard to forgive or love some people. However, if the Holy Spirit is in us, He will give us the grace and strength to do it when we ask Him.

Although David was pursued by King Saul and wanted to kill him for over 12 years: David's humility would not allow him to hate Saul, but rather he loved him and even spared his life twice. He had opportunities to kill Saul, during the period King Saul was trying to kill him but he knew that even though God had rejected King Saul as King over Israel, he knew it would not be right to kill him. Even if it meant the throne of Israel would be his.

How many of us would have the attitude of David? His warriors even did not understand him. But David knew God's Word; "vengeance is the Lord and he will repay" (Deuteronomy 32:35) and "do not touch my anointed ones" (Psalm 105:15, 1 Chronicles 16:22). David had such attitude of humility because the Word of God became so real to him.

God dwells in the praises of his people and since King David had this revelation it made him a worshiper, a lover of God and His Word. David also possessed an immensely forgiving heart.

We can also overcome un-forgiveness like King David when we allow the Scriptures and the Holy Spirit to convict our hearts. A humble heart easily forgives and reconciles with those who have offended them when they love and reverence God.

But stubborn hearts will be hardened. The knowledge of the Word of God and realizing the schemes of the devil are important if we are to defeat a spirit of un-forgiveness.

Un-forgiveness can also result in bitterness, resentment, diseases like cancer, heart and liver diseases etc. The cells of the human body literally begin to fight against themselves; weakening the immune system when there is un-forgiveness. Instead of repairing or rebuilding itself, your body can be hurt, get bitter, resentful, self-defensive and even cause you to socially withdraw from others.

Medical sciences show that an unforgiving heart affects blood vessels because the heart beats faster than usual. It automatically affects blood pressure. In the long run, cells in the body fight against themselves instead of defending your immune system. The immune system becomes weak and the body is vulnerable to diseases.

On the other hand, forgiveness can lower stress, lower blood pressure, reduce depression according to an article in Healthy Lifestyle dated August 3, 2010.

But un-forgiveness is deadly! It can kill both physically and spiritually; and worst of all it can lead to eternal death. God wants us to forgive freely, "unless we forgive those who have sinned against us, He will not forgive us our sins" (Matthew 6:14).

King David showed humility in his heart when he and Bathsheba were exposed in their sins. He displayed his humility in the tearing of his garment before God. He also fasted for the sick child that was born to him and Bathsheba out of wedlock. But God did not heal his son and allowed him to die as part of David's punishment. Yet, David was relentless, repented and received God's compassion when he and Bathsheba conceived a son they called Solomon, or Jedediah; meaning loved by God.

Through all of this, God was showing David who He is. He is Holy; He is just, merciful and a compassionate God. David's repentance was truly from his heart and not just from his lips. God likes people who sincerely repent from their hearts and not just from their lips.

The rendering of your garment in the Jewish culture means repentance. God wants us to render our hearts and not our garment, which means God wants true repentance that comes from the heart (the inner man) and reflects in your actions.

Hopefully, your actions would be motivated by a pure heart. You may fast to humble yourself before God but maybe with the wrong motives. You may afflict yourself in times of fasting; suffering physically, mentally and emotionally, but how much spiritual benefit is it?

Humbleness, or meekness, is one of the fruit of the Spirit mentioned in the book of Galatians. "Gentleness (meekness, humility), self-control (self-restraint, continence), against such things there is no law that can bring a charge that each believer definitely needs" (Galatians 5:23).

I encourage you to cry to God to show you His way and how to surrender your will to Him. The more you trust and obey God the easier it is to be humbled.

Old Testament saints knew very little about the Holy Spirit compared to the New Testament dispensation. Perhaps they knew little or nothing about the "fruit of the spirit", however; those who loved, obeyed and trusted in God automatically "walked in the spirit" or experienced God's presence.

Everyone that walks in the spirit must have a humble and teachable spirit to access God's Spirit. The Spirit of God is gentle. He does not like pride. How often do we experience pride without even noticing it before God speaks through someone or the Holy Spirit and convicts us?

The praises of men can easily distract us into pride. We live in a world full of deceptive people. There are so many distractions and deceptions around us. People are always hungry and desiring for something new. Others are searching for personalities or talents to idolize. Many are even easily being deceived about the how, when, and why of the coming of Christ!

A willingness to be humble before God will help you to avoid many painful deceptions in life. But sometimes God has to humble you when you have hardened your heart beyond the time of expired grace.

David had many opportunities to brag to King Saul and his fellow citizens about decapitating Goliath the giant, but he did not.

The Israelites women made songs out of David's success but he cared less about that (1 Samuel 18:7, 29:5). He knew promotion comes from God and the ability for success comes not by power nor by might but by the Spirit of God (Psalm 75:5-7).

God humbled King Nebuchadnezzar because of pride. He turned him into an animal (Daniel 4:33). God humbled King Pharaoh with the ten plagues of Egypt and after that he and his chariots were swallowed by the Red Sea (Exodus 14:28).

We must remember these stories of humility. Otherwise when we make a massive achievement in life or experience the success of our labor; we often retreat or relax and let the devil come and steal. We may give too much credit to ourselves, lose focus and lose sight of the need for humility.

David was promoted by God as a result of his humility. David's physical stature alone could have disqualified him as a King; he was short, around five feet four inches, but was God's chosen king.

Some people may be prideful at times; because of riches, career or family background. However, if you have the same mindset as David, I think you would discover the secret of a simple life.

David wrote "The Earth is the LORD'S and everything in it. The world and all that live in it" (Psalm 24:1). He understood this simple theology; God created all things and all that we have is

God's. He has given all things to us for the sake of His Kingdom and He could take all back at any given time.

How does this speak to you personally? Are you humble with your position, in your marriage, with your business, as a parent, or in your ministry?

If these questions are convicting you of a prideful heart, then I believe this little book will cause you to come out of the closet. I believe it is a season of repentance and restoration.

Please realize that God will not promote a prideful person. People who think they're already at the top of the world do not need to be elevated. He promotes those who know that they are low and need to be elevated.

Humbleness is not Poverty

However, being lowly or "poor in spirit" has nothing to do with poverty. This is another deception of the devil that has fooled unbelievers and believers alike. Some Christians believe poverty and humility are somehow linked together. What does the Scripture teach us about Christ and our poverty? Doesn't Scripture say the Lord became poor so that we might be rich?

The biblical definition of being rich deals with more than having a desirable financial status. In a Kingdom mindset, you become rich in your soul and the result of that prospers every area of your life, your health, finances, relationships etc.

Prospering in your soul leads to having a Kingdom mindset. Having a Kingdom mindset is having a heart and mind that is concerned about advancing the Kingdom of God. God wants us to be rich in our soul and in every area of life so that we possess the tools to advance His Kingdom; taking dominion over the earth!

Jesus exchanged His riches for our poverty "He was rich but became poor so that we might be rich through His death" (2 Corinthians 8:9). God doesn't want us to be lazy and live in lack so we do not have food to eat, clothing to wear, or a place to live.

At the same time He does not want us to "follow money." Money should follow us. We must follow God, seeking Him with all that we are or have then the riches of this world will follow us. Christ should be the center of the heart of every child of God. As the Lord Jesus taught the disciples "But seek first the kingdom of God and His righteousness, and all these things shall be added to you" Matthew 6:33).

There are many who are wealthy and humble while there are those who are prideful with their wealth. On the other hand, there are many extremely poor who consider their poverty a good thing. Even if God were to send them an Angel to help them financially they might turn it down.

God is abundant and purposeful. His heart is about Kingdom advancement and increase. He wants us to be blessed so that we would be positioned to help others. It is not about selfish ambitions as we read in the parable of the rich fool;

"And one of the company said unto him, Master, speak to my brother, that he divide the inheritance with me."

And he said unto him, Man, who made me a judge or a divider over you? And he said unto them, Take heed, and beware of covetousness: for a man's life consisteth not in the abundance of the things which he possesseth.

And he spoke a parable unto them, saying, The ground of a certain rich man brought forth plentifully:

And he thought within himself, saying, what shall I do, because I have no room where to bestow my fruits? And he said, this will I do: I will pull down my barns, and build greater; and there will I bestow all my fruits and my goods. And I will say to my soul, Soul, thou hast much goods laid up for many years; take thine ease, eat, drink, and be merry. But God said unto him, Thou fool, this night thy soul shall be required of thee: then whose shall those things be, which thou hast provided? So is he that layeth up treasure for himself, and is not rich toward God (Luke 12: 13-21, KJV).

I think God wants us to be productive workers and prospering financially as well as every other area in our life. We just need to know the proper balance of investing in the Kingdom of God and investing in the material things of this world. We live in a dual world, both spiritual and material. It takes God's wisdom and plan for your life to know the right balance of where to place the prosperity of your life to advance God's plan for you and His Kingdom.

King David was also wealthy and amassed most of his riches from victories over his enemies. He fought many battles and many wars through his lifetime and conquered many nations. It made David and Israel very prosperous.

They would capture all the gold, silver, cattle and all other good things of the land including the people whom they took as slaves. Despite David's enormous wealth it did not destroy his humility. He understood that he could not do anything without God. Sometimes we think we do not need God because we have all we need. But that is not a good practice.

David wrote in the book of Psalms 14 and 53 that the fool says in his heart that there is no God.

We can also read his own words from the scripture about his generous giving towards the Temple. "Moreover, because I have set my affection on the house of my God, I have given to the house of my God, over and above all that I have prepared for the holy house, my own special treasure of gold and silver: Three thousand talents of gold, of the gold of Ophir, and seven thousand talents of refined silver, to overlay the walls of the houses" (1 Chronicles 29:1-4).

The cost of building Solomon's Temple was estimated more than $174 billion in today's monetary value. That is an enormous amount of money for any building project! If the Temple was rebuilt at the cost of $174 billion today, would the world or the church protest that the price is to exorbitant?

Abraham, Isaac, Joseph and all those great men and women of old were humble, but most of them were wealthy. If the greatest men and women of the Bible were wealthy why should it be a sin for believers today to have wealth? Yes, with a willing and generous heart we are to offer all our life and at the same time God also wants us to enjoy what He has given us.

A thorough study of the Scriptures bears out that it is God who gives you the power to be wealthy (Deuteronomy 8:18). Your mindset or motives are the determining factor whether you will be a good steward of your wealth or not.

There is no room in the Kingdom to pursue riches by cheating or exploiting people, or to be a braggart. But there is a plentiful supply of riches and wealth in God's Kingdom to transform lives and advance the Kingdom of the gospel.

What are your motives for wealth and do you have the right mindset? Let us consider the following scriptures about King David and one of Jesus' Apostles, John.

"Let them shout for joy, and be glad, that favor my righteous cause: yea, let them say continually, Let the LORD be magnified, which hath pleasure in the prosperity of his servant" (Psalm 35:27). The Apostle John wrote "Beloved I pray that you may prosper in every way and that your body may keep well even as I know your soul keeps well and prospers" (3 John1:29, Amp).

From this context we see that it is God's intent that we prosper in our spiritual life, ministries, marriages, finances, relationships, etc. But the devil is deceitful; a thief who comes to steal, kill and destroy. He can twist the truth. How can we advance the Kingdom of God like King David did; feeding the hungry, clothing the naked, helping the needy, the poor, orphans, sending missionaries to the nations, and taking territories if we live in lack and poverty? It is time the body of Christ comes out of religious piety.

David was a wealthy king, but he kept his focus on God. He made God the center of his life. He always gave God the glory and testified how God prospered and made him successful. He did this without apology or fear of criticism. It is not always easy to give all the glory to God when riches, wealth and success are in abundance. I really like how NFL quarterback Tim Tebow expresses his faith.

"I look at it as a relationship that I have with Him [God] that I want to give Him the honor and glory anytime I have the opportunity. And then right after I give Him the honor and glory, I always try to give my teammates the honor and glory. And that's how it works because Christ comes first in my life, and then my family, and then my teammates."

Perhaps a better term for the world to understand is that we should give God all the "credit" for our successes. Most of the time we want to take credit for our achievements. That was not David's heart. Pride will always show up when we take the credit for ourselves.

God found a man in David who was humble enough to handle riches. Are you willing to be one of those like David; if not, why?

When you are ready to be a humble vessel of God, He will make use of your gifts and talents and areas of influence in your life. Whether your talents are at the forefront or behind-the-scenes, you are divinely positioned to be in a place of prosperity.

Whatever circles of life you live in, you have the potential to influence and affect others. What is your influence on those around you?

King David was talented in playing the harp and his gift of music was the source of his favor with King Saul. But it was not just the playing of the harp but also his character and humility that drew attention

Character versus Charisma

How often have you heard of a famous athlete, movie star or politician who is extremely gifted in their profession, but at the same time trouble seems to follow them? In most cases it probably had something to do with their character. This is why character is more important than your charisma or gifts. Character will determine how far your gifts will take you.

For example, you might be extremely gifted in shooting a gun. You might be able to hit the bull's-eye from a hundred yards away. But all that gifting and charisma will not take you to success if your character leads you to rob a bank. Staying humble in our gifts (charisma) is crucial.

You might believe that charisma is more important than character. Charisma is the grace or power of God that is possessed in your gifting. Our gifts may bring us to people of influence; however, without good character we probably will damage that relationship or opportunity.

In the book of Deuteronomy, God told the Israelites: "And thou shalt remember the LORD thou God for it is He that giveth thee power to get wealth, that may establish His covenant which He swore unto thy fathers unto this day" (Deuteronomy 8:18 KJV).

I believe King David might have also kept his shepherd's cloth to always remind himself of his past so that he would never exalt himself. We must not forget about our humble beginnings.

David praised God and remembered his humble beginning when God spoke to him concerning the building of the Temple. "Then King David went in and sat before the LORD; and he said: "Who am I, O LORD God? And what is my house, that you have brought me this far? (2 Samuel 7:18).

The story of Jacob is another outstanding example of humility. Jacob the son of Isaac and Rebecca had deceived his older brother Esau and had taken his birthright. Then he ran away to his uncle Laban, who in turn, deceived and cheated Jacob. But then Jacob would have to return to his older brother whom he ran from and had not seen in years.

Even though he knew his life was in danger by seeking out his brother Esau, he had to make amends with him. In his journey Jacob decided to spend the night by himself and found himself wrestling with the Angel of God (the Lord) till daybreak. And in this divine encounter, "the Lord touched the hollow of Jacob's thigh, and wrenched it out of its socket" (Genesis 32:31-32).

That was a memorial mark He gave Jacob. It would be a memorial of remembrance for the rest of his life. A life changing experience!

I think most of us need a mark to remind us of where God has to wrestle with our lives and establish memorials of remembrances.

34

However, in seeking to win the heart of God, humility helps us to avoid having to wrestle with God like Jacob.

Humility makes it easier to follow God's will rather than to try and wrestle Him before we realize He has the best plans in mind for us. Humility is the shorter path to get to our destination.

King David most often sought direction from God in assignments given to him (1 Samuel 23:1-2, 1 Samuel 30:8). David's humbleness was a key to following God's way of accomplishing His assignments instead of his own way. In his humility he was allowed to walk in close proximity with God which certainly made him transparent (Read the story in 2 Samuel 11, Psalm 51).

.Humility unlocks Promotion!

Humility is also one of the master keys to unlocking God's promotion. Humility attracts promotion. You may have heard the illustration that many teachers use about the constructing of tall buildings and the importance of their foundation.

In constructing tall buildings, the foundations have to be deep and strong so that they can hold the integrity of the building. If the foundation is not deep and strong a severe gust of wind could level the building.

A humble character is also the foundation stone that will allow you to reach to the full heights that God has planned for your life. God's divine plan for your life is going to require an understanding of God's word and a humble character before you decide to yield to His plan. Most of us are proud that we ventured through life making decisions by ourselves.

It's so easy for us to make our own decisions without consulting God for the divine plan. Do you know that at least fifty percent of college graduates do not use their degrees to get a job when they graduate?

Why? Because most of them made their decisions based on everything and anything except the foundation of humility and "Winning the Heart of God."

In your spiritual life, if you humble yourself before God, you can expect being lifted up and being promoted! That is His promise! Those who humble themselves before God shall inherit the earth. People of humble spirit reverence God. God reveals His secrets to those who fear Him like King David. "For the secret of the LORD is with them that fear Him, and He will show them His covenant" (Psalm 25:14), a Psalm of David.

Yes, God is merciful and causes the sun to shine on all—both the righteous and the unrighteous; however, there is understanding and revelation that He is only willing to unveil to those that fear Him. David was that kind of a man. He perceived his own weaknesses and strengths. He weighed both and came to a conclusion that the Lord is his strength, For He had become his salvation (Psalm 27:1-2). He admitted that he was conceived in sin and born as a sinner, and therefore he needed a Savior. He came to the end that "I cannot do this on my own." It is my prayer that as you are reading this book, you also surrender your life completely to God.

As we further delve into the meaning of humility, we find that a humble heart is a teachable heart. We can find several synonyms relating to a teachable heart when we look at the life of David.

Someone who is teachable is thirsty for knowledge and ripe for instruction. A prideful heart refuses instruction because it already thinks it is smart.

Have you ever purchased something from the store and tried to assemble it without the instruction manual? How often have you followed your own directions until you realized you had to disassemble it and start all over again? In the end, it took you twice as long to accomplish the task. Scripture says "fools despise wisdom and instruction" (Proverbs 1:7).

King David was thirsty for knowledge and wisdom. He learned to listen for God's voice before using his own wisdom. Let's examine several scriptures David wrote.

"Teach us to number our days so that we may gain a heart of wisdom" (Psalm 90:12).

"Show me, LORD, my life's end and the number of my days; let me know how fleeting my life is (Psalm 39:4).

I believe if we would slow down sometimes and think about our life, and how we use our precious time and days, we would certainly make some changes or adjustments. And this is especially true for the young. In our youth we are full of endless energy but short on practical experience.

Usually a parent or adult receive a flash-back as youth make decisions on adrenaline instead of with God or godly counsel. We realize how foolish we have been when we hit the wall after making the same mistakes of those who have gone before us.

David had the heart for God even in his youth. But his son Absalom did not learn from his father. He killed his half-brother Ammon for raping Tamar, Absalom's sister. David tried to restore his rebellious son, but in the end he was killed because of his own sins. King David hated sin but loved to forgive. He was a good listener and the doer of the word as a result of his teachable heart. And in the parable about the "wise and foolish builders," we also see that the wise builder was a humble and teachable person.

This is because he hears, listens and obeys God. "Therefore whoever hears these sayings of Mine, and does them, I will liken him to a wise man who built his house on the rock: and the rain descended, the floods came, and the winds blew and beat on that house; and it did not fall, for it was founded on the rock" (Matthew 7:24-25).

This is what a humble heart requires if you are to have a strong and solid foundation so that you will prosper in all that you do. They are like the palm trees planted by the streams of water, that bear fruits in and out of season.

"Blessed is the man that walketh not in the counsel of the ungodly, nor standeth in the way of sinners, nor sitteth in the seat of the scornful. But his delight is in the law of the LORD; and in his law doth he meditate day and night.

And he shall be like a tree planted by the rivers of water, that bringeth forth his fruit in his season; his leaf also shall not wither; and whatsoever he doeth shall prosper.

The ungodly are not so: but are like the chaff which the wind driveth away (Psalm 1:1-4 KJV).

Humility is a desirable trait that each one of us needs to develop in our life. It is a bodily posture which allows the Holy Spirit to develop your character so that you can have the mind of Christ (Philippians 2:5).

Jesus taught many lessons about humility through the topic of servant hood. How does humility and the heart of the servant relate? The mind of a servant understands humility. A servant does not have his own will, nor does a servant have his own reputation.

A servant even takes care of his master's needs before his own. A servant makes sure his master eats before he eats. He does not make his own opinion; but he obeys instructions even when he does not agree with his master. Our Lord said "Remember what I told you: A servant is not greater than his master" (John 15:20 NIV).

That was the Lord Jesus' nature. He loved and obeyed God even unto death on the cross. Will you examine your life right now to see who your master really is?

If you do not love Him with ALL your heart, then it means someone or something has taken His place in your heart. No one can serve two masters because you will love one and hate the other.

He also taught us to love one another. When we love one another we also practice humility. Humility and love focus outward towards others instead of inward towards ourselves.

"My command is: love each other as I have loved you" (John 15:12).

39

Loving and obeying the Lord develops the character of humbleness.

Personal Note

Things to Remember from Chapter 1

God opposes the proud and gives grace to the Humble.

God will not force us to obey His Word or do His will.

Humility is not poverty. There are people who are poor but prideful and there are others who are humble but wealthy.

Humility requires obedience; knowing that we cannot make it on our own and need God's help.

We cannot resist the devil if we do not know how to submit to God.

King David praised God with all his heart.

Chapter 2

Know the Power of Praise

Expressing your Gratitude

The words "Thank you" can be expressed in various ways. It is a courtesy. Being thankful means you are grateful, you have a heart of gratitude. You appreciate whatever service or deed has been offered to you. How do you express yourself when you are thankful to someone? Do you express it outwardly, opening your mouth... or just inwardly, keeping it to yourself though you know you should say something? I believe the proper way of being appreciative is to show it outwardly, not for people to see it per se, but for the person you're thankful to, to know you have a thankful heart.

How can someone know you are thankful if you don't express it? You should therefore express it to them in words unless you have a disability in speaking. However, expression speaks more than words as the saying goes, so even with a disability your thankful heart will be visible. Probably the best motive one should have is to be willing to express your heart openly but even if other people don't notice your heart or how appreciative you are, you do not really care.

Sometimes people try to be quiet instead of being vocal because of shyness or fear. This was not so with King David because he had the motive to express his gratitude to God before all men. He praised God with all his heart, mind, soul, and strength.

Many other words of expression come to mind when we hear the word "praise." One may think of such words as applaud, approval, express admiration for, and many more. However, to the people in the Judeo- Christian beliefs, we see something spectacular about the word "praise." In some of versions they used "bless" instead of "praise."

For instance in the book of Psalms (103, 147, 150) we see a lot of the word "praise." The word "praise" has a different translation however; I will use the Hebrew word "halel." The word "halel" is not only translated as "praise" but it is also translated as "shine" as in Job 29:3. The original meaning of "halel" is the North Star. This star, unlike all of the other stars, remains unmovable and continuously shines in the northern sky and throughout many years of history it was used as a guide or compass for travelers in the ancient times.

Therefore to the ancient Hebrew the word "halel" meant God is like the North Star, that He is the one to look to for direction. One of the letters with the ancient Hebrew writings showed a man with his hand lifted up, signifying something great. Certainly God is

42

great. He is indeed the greatest of all! Another one of the ancient Hebrew letters was one that looked like a shepherd's rod. It depicted how the shepherd led his flock.

This shows the character of God and His attributes; that the Lord God is immovable and unshakable. He is the light to your path as the Lord Jesus said that He is the light of the world. Truly, if you follow Him you will never walk in darkness so He is worthy to be praised. Do you believe that?

King David was from the tribe of Judah. Judah means praise. Judah was one of the twelve sons of Jacob or Israel (Genesis 29:35, 48:9). Therefore, it was no wonder that King David knew how to praise God. He was grateful to God all the time!

Because of his thankful heart King David assigned people who would praise God daily in the Temple 24/7 when he was planning for the construction of the temple. He did this because he had the understanding that God literally inhabits in the praises of His people!

For instance, one of the famous songs in the book of Psalms is Psalm 100. Here the Psalmist declared "Enter His gates with thanksgiving; enter His courts with praise." The Solomon Temple had three courts. First, the outer court, second the Holy place and then last, the Most Holy Place or Holy of Holiest. These three stages from my perspective are thanksgiving, praise and worship.

The Power of Praise.

The Psalmist taught us to enter His gates with thanksgiving. There were several gates that led to the Temple. Hence, before one entered the gates he believed their hearts and mouths should be

43

filled with thanksgiving. In the courts praise, exaltation, and thanksgiving should be offered to God. Praise normally goes with thankfulness; they are like twins. If you are familiar with twins you can relate to this. Either they move together or the moment you see one, the other would be following.

There are two altars in life; the altar of praise and the altar of lamentation. The altar of praise is where we praise God when things are going well. It is easy and fun to praise God when everything is going in what we believe is the right direction and our expectations are being met or exceeded. For instance, when our children are doing well in school, when we have good marriages, when our businesses are booming, or when we have a nice boss and the right colleagues to work with, etc. We find it easy to praise God during these times.

However, when the situation happens to be the opposite it is not so easy to praise God. Sometimes the storms of life can crush you down so much that if you do not lift your eyes up to the Lord who calms the storms, you will be drowned. Should you go through a series of storms like King David did the best thing to do is to cry out to God.

Don't deny your pain or loss. Go ahead and grieve it. Be honest about it and even be angry if you need to, but do not sin. Don't let the anger control you; tell you what to do, but instead you control your anger and tell it what to do!

Do not hit someone, or use abusive words, etc. Instead, be angry at the devil. Ultimately everything wrong goes back to him, but everything good comes from God. And when God allows bad things to happen to you like He allowed in the life of Job and other great men and women of God, it means that He sees something very good that will develop from out of the bad. When we choose to praise Him in it all but be angry at the devil, He sees it as worship for Himself.

We have to be transparent and pour out our hearts sincerely before God, but at the same time we should know how to praise Him in spite of our situations.

King David wrote fourteen Psalms that are related to specific life events in his own life. There was a time that King David had to flee from King Saul because of his evil acts and he lived in Gath, which was the territory of the Philistines, his enemies. His life was in danger and he wrote Psalm 56 through this life experience.

He wrote how God had even bottled up his tears. In the tenth verse he had even more confidence in Almighty God and His Word than he had before. He praised God and His Word because God's Word is unmovable.

Similarly, when you praise God you are telling Him that you acknowledge the good that He has done and that you are expecting even more from Him.

"Thou tellest my wanderings: put thou my tears into thy bottle: are they not in thy book? When I cry unto thee, then shall mine enemies turn back: this I know; for God is for me. In God will I praise His Word: in the LORD will I praise His Word" (Psalm 56:8-10, KJV).

King David wrote Psalms 34 which was related to the very situation discussed above. He had run away from his home and family because his life was threatened.

David was seeking refuge in Achish-Gath and the King of Achish Abimelech had heard that David was hiding in his city. His servants brought him to the King and David pretended to be insane by spitting on himself. Abimelech asked them to get David out of his sight because he was insane.

King David knew when to build the right altar at the right time. He wept whenever he needed to, but in spite of the weeping he would give God the glory and praise due to Him.

King David had a lot of opposition and enemies. We all have an enemy like King David had; the Bible says Satan is your enemy. "Be alert and of sober mind. Your enemy the devil prowls around like a roaring lion looking for someone to devour" (1 Peter 5:8). In Psalm 27, David wrote, "The Lord is my Light and my Salvation whom shall I fear?"

This was a season when he was in darkness. He knew the Lord is the Light of the world. Light travels at over 186,000 mile per second. Darkness cannot overcome light because light is greater than darkness. David said the Lord was his salvation and his deliverer.
We need a deliverer when we are in trouble; we need a savior when we are perishing. David praised God because He knew the power of praise. The more he praised God the more he saw the greatness of God compared to the strength of his enemies. From the seventh verse we see how he poured out his heart to God.

He cried out to God for mercy. Mercy is hope for sinners and a refuge for the righteous. Therefore, upon reading the entire verse we see that David praised God. He prayed, he lamented, but he was thankful to God. We see he was discouraged at some point that he would have lost heart for all the false witnesses against him. His life was in so much danger that only God could deliver him. Does this sound like your situation? King David had a thankful heart.

Here in the United States of America we have a Day of Thanksgiving. It is celebrated the fourth Thursday in November. It is a day set apart to be thankful to God. The pilgrims especially, who first came to the United States from Europe to settle here were thankful for all that God had done for them. Every year families gather together around their dining tables and celebrate with feasting. People share testimonies of how they are thankful to God and to the people around them.

It is also the season when most people remember their loved ones who have passed away and it can be really hard to be thankful to God possibly because of the sorrow. Grieving is a part of life and if we see it that way we will be able to praise God on both the altar of praise and on the altar of lamentation.

Learning to be thankful to God and praising Him even before we bring in our request is key not only to answered prayer, but in how it puts us in a posture that God can entrust us with more because He knows that we have faith in Him and that we will worship Him.

In one of David's songs he wrote "I will praise you as long as I live, lifting up my hands to you in prayer" (Psalms 63:4). He was willing to praise God as long as he lived! This meant whether he had abundance or not, whether he was sick or healthy. He purposed in his heart to praise God and nothing would stop him from doing so. Can you also make that confession?

The mind is the battle ground where all of our thoughts come in before they get into our hearts. The mind needs to be trained to meditate on things that are pure and true which will eventually affect our thoughts and perceptions. You can train your mind to meditate on the right things like you train your pet. You may get a scripture that relates to your situation and what the Word of God has said concerning you or your situation.

First of all you have to read, believe, and think about it. You must speak out those scriptures over and over till it registers in your mind,

The Scripture says the children of God should dance before Him with praise. "Praise His Name with dancing, accompanied by tambourine and harp" (Psalm 149:3).

I believe as you go before God with praise and dancing, thanking Him in advance of what you are expecting from Him, He will answer your prayers accordingly. I call this "Faith Dance."

Some people may praise God quietly because of shyness. The Lord Jesus said, if anyone is ashamed of Him in this sinful and adulterous generation, He will also be ashamed of him when He descends in His Father's glory with the holy angels (Mark 8:38).

King David understood the principles of royalty. He acknowledged God as the King of the universe. King David knew that God was the King over him, even as the Psalmist wrote "Let Israel rejoice in Him that made him; let the children of Zion be joyful in their King. Let them praise Him in the dance; let them

48

sing praises unto Him with timbrel and harp" (Psalm 149:2-3 KJV).

Kings delight in Entertainments.

Royalties and dignitaries know the importance of authority and submission (protocol), as in the story of the Centurion and his sick servant in the gospel of Luke (Luke 7:1-10). The Centurion came to the Lord with the request that his servant was sick and he needed healing. Because he was a man of authority and understood what it meant to be a leader, he asked the Lord to just say the word and his servant would be healed. The Lord honored his request and his servant was healed.

Not only does God want His children to praise Him, He wants every instrument and everything that has breath to praise Him. "Praise Him with the timbrel and dance; praise Him with stringed instruments and organs. Let everything that has breath praise the LORD. Praise the LORD" (Psalm 150:4,6).

Kings delight in entertainment. One of the sad stories in the Bible is the death of John the Baptist.

King Herod promised with an oath to give Herodias' daughter whatever she would ask.

King Herod the Tetrarch who was a Sub-King in Judea imprisoned John the Baptist for speaking against his adulterous lifestyle. He had divorced his wife and married Herodias, the wife of his brother Herod Philip. On Herod the Tetrarch's birthday, Herodias daughter danced to entertain his guests and because he wanted to please his guests he demanded that the head of John the Baptist should be

49

given to the young lady because that was her request (Mark 6:14-29).

Some of the early disciples were martyred while being used as entertainment instruments by wicked leaders like Emperor Nero of Rome and others. They delighted to see the believers screaming and praising God in hot waters, fire, or oil till they were dead. Some too delighted to hear the wild animals (lions) breaking the bones of the believers. That was their entertainment.

When Daniel was cast into the lions' den, the King could not have his entertainment that night because he knew Daniel was a righteous man (Daniel 6:18). His story was an outstanding one. God knows why He saves some who go through persecution, but allows others to die. However, He always uses the bad or evil for His good plans and purposes.

The Kings in our present day also like entertainment however, in a different form; certainly not through murdering others. Therefore King David understood the delights of Kings. King David acknowledged God as King, and of course King above all kings.

He paid homage to Him, and danced before Him as minor Kings often did before major Kings (2 Samuel 6:14). Remember, you're a King and a Priest, therefore dancing before God should not be strange (Revelation 1:6, 5:10).

King David had a childlike faith and danced like a child before his parent. His wife despised him for dancing almost naked because she did not know the heart of her husband. He danced before God because his dream of bringing the Ark or the presence of God to Israel was fulfilled.

The Ark of the Covenant was captured by the Philistines even before Saul became a King. They later sent it to Abinadad's house for about twenty years (2 Samuel 6:2-3). Then it was given to Obed-Edom for about three months to take care of because most of the Israelites including King David were afraid to bring it near them.

God instructed them about how to carry the ark. Unfortunately they wanted to do it their own way and that resulted in the death of Uzzah who wrongfully touched the ark. God really prospered Obed-Edom for taking care of the Ark of the Covenant. When King David heard about that he went to fetch it from Obed-Edom (1 Chronicles 13:14). The ark represented the presence of God, which means that all that time when Israel was without the Ark, they were without the presence of God. Can you catch the glimpse of why King David was so excited that he danced like he had lost his mind? I don't want to exchange the presence of God for anything!

Quite a few people go to Church especially on Sundays feeling shy or afraid to clap their hands in praise and worship. Meanwhile they may go to the clubs on Saturday nights and dance for hours. Then they present themselves in a sanctimonious way before Him on Sunday. That is false humility.

How is it possible to praise God in silence? The Psalmist wrote "O come, let us sing unto the LORD, let us make a joyful noise unto the rock of our Salvation, Let us come before His presence with thanksgiving and make a joyful noise unto Him with Psalms" (95:1-2, Ps 98:6, 100:1-2).

We make a joyful noise unto God because He delights in it. Joyful noise is completely different than any ordinary noise, as we could see the adjective qualifying the noun. Joyful noises were common in Bible times, especially after wars. Whenever, a nation conquered another, the triumphal nation would bring their captives as well as the spoils or booty to their own lands.

A messenger would go ahead of them to announce the victory and the women would sing with a joyful noise to meet them at the gates of the city and they would walk across the city to display their victory with the booty and the captives. The Apostle Paul wrote "And having disarmed the powers and authorities, He made a public spectacle of them triumphing over them by the cross" (Colossians 2:15).

That was what the Lord did to Satan and his kingdom through His death and resurrection. This shows how vital joyful noise and praises are. Satan and his demons become paranoid and hide just like a snail or tortoise coils into its shell. Joyful noise and praising God means we are the winners; it shows that we know our identity and position.

We hold on to our perspective as conquerors and more that conquerors in Christ Jesus. We are admonished to clap our hands and shouts unto God with a voice of triumph (Psalm 47:1).

This Psalm was written just about the Assyrian invasion of Judah by King Sennacherib (2 Kings 18:13-19:37). God intervened in that situation and turned things around in the favor of the people of

Judah. The Assyrian King was killed by his own son and Judah was freed from their threat.

There is another familiar story in the Old Testament about King Jehoshaphat and the people of Judah. They were surrounded by the Moabites, the Ammonites, and the people from Mount Seir. The Moabites and Ammonites were the descendants of Lot, the nephew of Abraham.

They surrounded Judah, or the Southern kingdom, with the intent of destroying them and their lands even though God had already warned them not to touch them. King Jehoshaphat and the people of Judah praised God and fasted and God fought on their behalf (2 Chronicles 20).

King David was a song writer and instrumentalist, a worshiper who could be in the presence of God for a long time. He was someone who could fast just because he was desperate for more of God. There were all kinds of possibilities for worship he was not ashamed to dance before the Lord anytime he felt like. The story of the Ark of the Covenant was mentioned because it was a solemn moment for the nation of Israel.

Will you dance like King David danced when the Spirit of the Lord comes upon you? I believe the greatest entertainment we could ever give to God is to dance in His presence with all of our hearts and strength.

Praise is a weapon of war you need to silent your enemy, the devil. If the devil can keep you silent from praising God he can disarm you and render you powerless!

Personal Notes.

Pray without ceasing (I Thess 5: 17)

Lesson 3

Prayer- A Spiritual Exercise!

There is a popular reference to prayer that says "MORE PRAYER, MORE POWER LESS PRAYER LESS POWER."

It is commonly believed that prayer is the "key" or "master key" that unlocks heavenly treasures. Whether it is the key or the master key, prayer has more power than any weapon of war imagined. Prayer should never be under estimated. However, at the same time you may find prayer to be the hardest thing on earth to do.

Prayer literally means talking, fellowshipping or communicating with God. God is a Personal Being just like Jesus was when He came and walked on the earth. The Holy Spirit, the Third Person of the Trinity is also a Person. (Trinity = Triune God: God the

Father, Son and the Holy Spirit (John 14:26, Matthew 28:19). Every personal being has emotions, a will, and an intellect.

The song writer Joseph Scriven wrote "What a friend we have in Jesus... what a privilege to carry everything to God in prayer." It is God's desire that we come to Him just as we go to our earthly parents with our requests or problems, expecting and believing that He is capable and willing to help us.

There are always three answers we should expect from God: Yes, No, or Wait.

God answers us whenever we pray to Him, though it might not be the answer we expect. His answer can be encouraging, or a direction for our life, a rebuke, a charge, or even an assignment we are expected to accomplish.

David was a man of prayer. He was continually seeking the Lord. He was always hungry for more of God and he used his harp to draw closer to Him. He had a natural passion for the heartbeat of God. God's heart is restoring and redeeming lost souls who will forsake their unrighteous ways and turn to him.

Secondly, God grants justice to the oppressed because justice and righteousness are the foundations of His throne. Psalms 89:14 shows how King David trusted the Lord with all his heart. He also had the revelation that the higher your position in office, the greater your responsibilities; he who much is given much is expected (Luke 12:48).

David probably started writing his songs which are recorded in the book of Psalms while a shepherd in the wilderness. He prayed for God's protection over his life and his sheep. The well known 23rd

Psalm was written by David and says "The Lord is my Shepherd I shall not want." The "not want" means lacking nothing!

Through his prayer and devotion, David had such confidence in his relationship with God that he wasn't afraid to even fight the giant Goliath. He knew it was not by his "might nor by power, but by the spirit of God" (Zech 4:6). God is our source of strength.

The more we pray the more we build an intimate relationship with the Holy Spirit. The more we know the revelation of God, the greater things we can accomplish, because the Word of God says that those who know their God will be strong and do exploits (Daniel 11:32).

King David experienced a "revelation knowledge" of the Lord Jesus through the Spirit of God. Even though Jesus had not yet come in the flesh in the Old Testament, we can gain an understanding of this through the Scriptures. What is revelation knowledge? It is divine information (insights, direction and mysteries) you can receive from God when you listen to him in prayer and meditation.

The book of Psalms illustrates prophetic Scriptures that validate this. We read in the book of Psalms; "The LORD says to my Lord, sit at my right hand until I make your enemies a footstool for your feet."

My "LORD" in that context, means the Lord God Almighty or Yahweh. "Lord" also represents Lord and Savior Jesus. This does not diminish the Sovereignty of our Lord Jesus. He was God before creation just as the Apostle John wrote "In the beginning was the Word and the Word was with God and the Word was God" (John 1:1).

David experienced a "revelation knowledge" of the Savior of the world. Much of this revelation is expressed prophetically through the Old Testament and realized through the New Testament that He (Jesus) is the exact image of God, therefore whoever sees Him has seen the Father and He and the Father are one.

King David had insight through the Spirit of God, just as Simon Peter was able to recognize the divinity of Jesus. When Jesus asked Simon Peter who do you say that I am, he replied, "You are the Christ, the Son of the Living God."

And the Lord answered him, "Blessed are you Simon Bar-Jonah, for flesh and blood has not revealed this to you, but my Father who is in Heaven" (Matthew 16:16-17).

We can also read from the gospel of Luke about a conversation Jesus had with some of the Jews:

And He said to them, "How can they say that the Christ is the Son of David? Now David himself said in the Book of Psalms:

'The LORD said to my Lord, "Sit at My right hand, Till I make Your enemies Your footstool." Therefore David calls Him 'Lord'; how is He then his Son?" (Luke 20:41-44).

The more you are dedicated to God in prayer, the more revelation knowledge you get from Him. You need insight for direction in life, for help with your family, your community etc.

It is said that revelation knowledge is not taught, it is caught. For example, if you have never met your father before and you were calling him on the phone for the first time, the best way for you to get knowledge of who he is would be by talking to him and knowing his voice.

This is the way revelation knowledge works. The more you draw near to God in prayer, the easier it is to hear from Him. God is ready and willing to reveal to you His Spirit and power when you make yourself available to Him. He gives you power (anointing) to do His will and to realize your destiny in life.

He does not want you to go through life without the power of the anointing because you cannot do His will without it. The anointing power will come on you and give you the ability to do great exploits. The anointing is also called the favor of God. The more you set yourself apart to seek God, the more He pours His anointing on you to do supernatural feats.

The Bible is filled with men and women who had walked in the supernatural. But it wasn't necessarily because they were special people. We all have favor to accomplish the supernatural.

In the Old Testament book of Judges we find the familiar story about Samson. Samson was physically strong. God used him as a mighty judge to bring deliverance to the Israelites during the rule of the Judges (Judges 13-16).

He was born a Nazarite. Nazarites normally took vows not to cut their hair, drink alcohol or fermented drinks. (Please know a Nazarite is not necessarily from the city of Nazareth). This was done to set themselves apart for consecration to the Lord (Numbers 6:1-21).

God anointed him to deliver the Israelites from the oppression of their enemy the Philistines, but the love of a woman became his downfall. He was seduced by a prostitute who betrayed him to the Philistines.

The Philistines gouged both of his eyes out and made him a slave. However, God is merciful, and gives second chances, even third or more when you fall or sin. For instance, in the story of Samson he cried out to God in prayer and God heard him and grant him victory over his enemies at the end of his life though he didn't live long.

The more you seek God, the more you find Him. The more you seek Him the more you will discover "Winning the Heart of God." He is not too far from any one of us.

God knew King David's heart that he was desperate for more of Him, not for his own selfish desires or ambitions, but for building God's kingdom.

How could God deny David of His Spirit and power when he was desperate for Him? God would not deny him. Neither will He deny you if you are desperate. The hunger and thirst in David's heart for more of the Spirit of God could not be hidden from God. As a result of pursuing God, prayer became a part of him.

Prayer or communicating with God should be your lifestyle. It really requires determination to experience the Spirit and power of God. You have to purpose it in your mind and heart like King

David and pursue it. He purposed in his heart to pray or fellowship with God each day of his life.

David's intimate pursuit of God went unnoticed until God sent the Prophet Samuel to anoint David as king. God had rejected King Saul as King over Israel and David, just a small shepherd boy was in the field tending his father's sheep when the Prophet arrived to speak to his father Jesse.

Jesse and the Prophet Samuel never had in mind who God would choose to be the next King. They might have thought it was the oldest son because the oldest normally inherited the birthright in Jewish culture. David was the youngest and was despised among his own family. Just a teenager, he was short compared to his brothers who were all tall and stout.

Samuel's choice was to anoint Jesse's older son because of his stature, but God said "No." Jesse lined up all of his sons, except David. But God said "No" to each of them. David was out in the field tending sheep at that time because no one expected him to be the chosen one anyway. God told Samuel that man looks on the outward appearance but He looks into the heart (1 Samuel 16:7).

Samuel asked Jesse to send for David, and when he arrived, God told Samuel to anoint him. God had David on His mind and was His choice to be the King even though he was shunned as the black sheep of his family.

Does David's story remind you of a time when you were rejected as the black sheep in your family or community because of something you did in the past? Please know that "God takes despised things and things that are not, to confound the things that are" (1 Corinthians 1:27).

God will take your mess and turn it into a wonderful "message" so you have a personal story to share with those who need the good news. You have to believe in the word and promises of God when you pray like King David. You will then see the fruit of your prayers also.

David's heart as a shepherd is wonderfully illustrated in Scripture. Shepherds are normally tenderhearted, patient, loving, and caring people and so the Prophet Jeremiah refers to the Israelites spiritual leaders as shepherds several times in his book.

For instance, he wrote "And I will give you shepherds according to My heart, who will feed you with knowledge and understanding" (Jeremiah 3:15, NKJV).

Unlike a hired hand, the good shepherd will not run away when wolves or ferocious animals attack. He will defend and protect the sheep. A good shepherd will take care of his sheep. He will not even leave one behind; therefore David depended on God's daily protection for the flock. David probably learned to position himself in continual prayer because he lived in the wilderness exposed to wild animals all the time.

As David spent many hours in the wilderness with his sheep he had plenty of opportunities to reflect on and learn about the images of life-giving water. This was the source of many of his popular writings in the book of Psalms.

He understood the importance of getting fresh water for his sheep and he also knew that the Lord is the "Living Water" that shall never run dry.

King David was taught from the Torah since his infancy how God gave the Israelites fresh water in the wilderness. A loving and a tender hearted shepherd will take his sheep to the green pastures.

Often a shepherd has to travel to a distant region to find green pastures. David had to be willing to travel that distance and even risk his life at times for the life of his sheep. This is the picture of the Lord who also was willing to sacrifice His life on the cross on our behalf.

He knew the Lord is the Good Shepherd. The Lord was his source of protection, provision and the only way for him to be prosperous. I believe these life experiences caused him to pray continually.

We also see God told Joshua that he should not depart from the book of the law. He should meditate on them day and night, which were his steps to success and prosperity (Joshua 1:8).

King David was wise because he delighted in the Word of God. There were times he cried out to God, which literally means he prayed out loud to God; especially when he was in danger. Scripture records that he was in danger and snares of death many times.

While still a young shepherd boy he killed a lion and a bear before they could attack his flock. His life was in danger when King Saul wanted to kill him. He was in danger when his son Absalom rebelled and ousted him as King and took over the throne. However, God frustrated all the plans of the enemies of David.

Moses was also a shepherd before God called him as the leader of the Israelites to bring them out of slavery from Egypt to the Promised Land.

He learned the humble shepherd's life which helped to prepare him for leadership and to fulfill his life's purpose. Even though Scripture is silent about what Moses and David did while attending their sheep, they most undoubtedly communicated with God in prayer during many lonely nights out in the field.

David, Moses, and others were all forerunners to our Lord Jesus who was and is the ultimate example of the Good Shepherd who lays down His life for His sheep (John 10:11).

Jesus would indeed lay down His life. He too had to pray and be in communication with the Father just as all leaders need a life of prayer for wisdom to guide their congregations.

The Tabernacle and the Temple.

The book of Exodus tells us how God led Moses and the Hebrew slaves through the desert with great signs and wonders. But He also made Himself known through the Tabernacle. The Tabernacle was how the Spirit of God manifested Himself. This is how God would dwell with His people for forty years in the desert and on into the Promised Land.

Then when David became King, the Lord gave him a vision to build a temple that would eventually be built by his son Solomon. The Temple was built by Jews and pagans alike and it was to be a prayer house for "ALL NATIONS."

It then became God's dwelling place and there the Priests would come and listen to God's voice and be in His presence. Hence, only the High Priests could come into the presence of God in those days.

But the Tabernacle and the Temple were also just the forerunner of what was to come for God's people. God did not intend for His Spirit to dwell in buildings and temples, but with the hearts of His people. God had a plan to live within and to constantly commune with every one of His children. So, God's people would become the dwelling place of His Spirit. No more would a special Priest have to represent you before God.

Now you can be the dwelling place of God's Spirit. You can go to God in prayer and commune with him within your own spirit. Now you can pray without ceasing by talking to God personally. God wants us to talk to Him, believing Him for protection, receiving forgiveness of sins, and any other petitions that concerns us.

The model of the Tabernacle and the Temple helps us to see how different forms of prayer are available to us today. We can learn much from how David communicated with God in the days of the Temple. He wrote "I was glad when they said unto me, Let us go into the house of the LORD" (Psalm 122:1).

King David knew and believed in the importance of prayer, whether it was individual or congregational. Israel did not have the Temple in his days, since his son built it after his death.

The children of Israel also had the Tabernacle. A Tabernacle in the Hebrew language means a dwelling place or residence. It was a tent made to keep the Ark of the Covenant which represented the presence of God. Unlike the Temple that was for ALL NATIONS the Tabernacle was built by Jews, for Jews to worship God. It was taken from place to place as Israel moved from one location to another. It was built by the Jews for worship, prior to the building of the Solomon's Temple.

We learn that our body is the temple of the Holy Spirit in the New Testament, because God's Spirit lives in us (1 Corinthians 6:19). We are therefore taught from the scriptures to carry the presence of God wherever we go. King David also tried to faithfully represent the presence of God wherever he went.

He knew how to go to God in prayer, not only in the Tabernacle, but wherever he was. While being pursued by King Saul for several years, running from place to place and cave to cave; there was no way for him to meet with his family or go to the Tabernacle, hence he called on the LORD wherever he was.

He had the revelation that God is Omnipresent, so he could pray to Him or worship Him anywhere and at all times. This is why Jesus told the woman at the well "we don't have to go to the mountains or to Jerusalem to worship God" (John 4:21-24), because the Jews used to go to the mountains to pray. This is the attitude you should strive for as you worship God in spirit and in truth.

King David's plans for the Temple was for it to be a center for non-stop prayer and worship house. Communion with God should be with the attitude of a humble heart. We have to be transparent. David said "Search me, O God, and know my heart! Try me and know my thoughts! (Psalm 139:23)

He also wrote "May the words of my mouth the meditation of my heart be pleasing in Your sight, O LORD, my Rock and my Redeemer" (Psalm 19:14). The level of our intimacy with the Lord is in proportion to our reverence and love for Him. The more we love God the more we will trust Him.

Do you want to know the secrets of God? Then learn how to reverence Him. Prayer is an avenue of intimacy to get you closer to Him. In one of King David's songs he wrote "The fool says in his heart there is no God" (Psalm 14:1). In the Hebrew it is more pointedly stated, "The fool hath said in his heart, 'No, God!'"

Many still do not believe that God exists, against all evidence. They would not believe even if someone rose from the dead. It is sad to see people like sheep without a shepherd; they are in desperate need of the Savior of the world.

The Apostle Paul admonished the saints in Thessalonica to pray without ceasing" (Thessalonians 15:17). Jesus also encourages us with the parable of the persistent widow in the Gospel of Luke; "...always pray and not turn coward (faint, lose heart) and give up" (Luke 18:1, Amp).

To pray without ceasing means to be in a constant attitude of prayer. However, God does not want us to be on our knees the whole day and night. It does mean you should be in the spirit and in constant fellowship with Him through His Spirit.

Prayer certainly is one of the ways we are protected from temptation, prayer keeps us from losing confidence, even as the Lord taught in the Lord's prayer, "And lead us not into temptation, but deliver us from the evil one"(Matthew 6:13).

The Lord Jesus is our model to follow; if He prayed daily and many times through the night, you will also have that opportunity. Have you ever thought about how he prayed in the garden just before His crucifixion? Being in agony (of mind) He prayed (all the) more earnestly and intently, and His sweat became like great clots of blood dropping down to the ground, (Luke 22:44, Amp).

The scriptures also tell us how He drove the people out of the Temple because it was being wrongfully used. The Temple or God's house is to be reverend and used as a house of prayer.
"Then Jesus went into the Temple of God and drove out all those who bought and sold in the Temple, and overturned the tables of the money changers and the seats of those who sold doves. And He said to them, "It is written, 'My house shall be called a house of prayer,' but you have made it a 'den of thieves.'" (Matthew 21:12-13).

But the average Christian prays less than thirty minutes a day. This gives Satan an open door to attack God's children. Prayer is vital for every believer, because without intimacy there is no relationship with God.

This is what makes many marriages fail today. How would you feel if your spouse did not talk to you for several days? Would you feel rejected, not loved? Do you think, maybe he or she might be seeing or dating someone else?

You hurt God each time you choose not to speak to Him in prayer, but only cry out in time of trouble. You cannot manipulate God and make Him your sugar daddy. He is God, Holy and Almighty. The reason that you and I live is to worship Him, and if you miss your purpose, He can cause the stones to worship Him as He testified to the Pharisees.

"And some of the Pharisees from the throng said to Jesus, reprove your disciples. He replied, I tell you that if these keep silent, the stones will cry out" (Luke19:39-40).

God wants us to talk to Him. He loves to hear our voices daily, just as parents enjoy talking with their kids. Communication in relationship is so vital that we cannot ignore it, for there is no relationship without communication. Some people have been disconnected from their earthly parents or children and they carry hurt in their hearts that hinders their spiritual life and personal relationship with God.

Many who have been hurt by their earthly fathers have transferred that hurt to their relationship with God. Many who have been hurt by their own mothers have problems with compassion and have a hard time understanding what comfort is. It makes it hard to hear the gentle voice of the Holy Spirit, our Comforter.

Lastly, God's image has also been distorted through sibling rivalry. Sometimes our relationships as brothers and sisters in Christ may not always function as they should. You may have a hard time seeing Jesus as your brother because He did not come to your side through abuse or humiliation that you experienced.

God was certainly there, He saw it all, though it was not orchestrated by Him. He has the power to stop all evil, but there are reasons why He does not always intervene. I guess no one knows why He would allow some people go through horrible situations. I think the answer is simply that it is His discretion or decision because the Scripture says God is in Heaven and we are on the earth. He does whatever He pleases (Psalms 115:3,135:6).

Some people may go through hard times because of their wrong decisions. Sometimes it's wrong decisions from family members passed down through generations. If you don't understand your authority in Christ, you are vulnerable to generational curses. Through prayer and understanding of your authority in Christ you can prevent many bad experiences and every generational curse in the family could be turned into generational blessings.

Ignorance of Scripture may also be a reason why people go through hardships. God says His people perish for lack of knowledge (Hosea 4:6).

Others may go through hardship even though they are righteous like Job (Job chapter 1). God allowed Job to go through so many trials and temptations in spite of the fact that he was righteous. In the end God restored all that he had lost, doubled. I don't think anyone wants to go through such trials though there are rewards that come with it. God is in heaven and does whatever he wants on earth, but He is good and his mercies endure forever more.

In King David's case, he was guilty of adultery and murder; however the guilt drew him closer to God instead of pulling him away from God. Sometimes when you sin, you believe in the lies of the devil that you cannot be restored. The devil doesn't want you to live in the freedom and blessing that God has ordained for you. Jesus died so that if you believe in His name you would be freed from the power of the devil.

Prayer is truly one of the channels through which we walk in freedom. You might see prayer as just a religious exercise, but David had devoted himself to an intimate relationship with God through his prayer life. David knew how and when to pray.

Among the kinds of prayers that David regularly prayed were prayers of thanksgiving, of supplication, of intercession, and of repentance and worship. He also prayed militant prayers or spiritual warfare.

Thanksgiving prayer is where the prayers are solely thanking God for all that He has done for you.

Supplication prayer is where you bring your request or need to God.

Intercession prayer is where you bring other's requests and needs to God.

Repentance prayer is when we repent of our sins and that of others, for instance our family or nation, and ask God for forgiveness.

Knowing how to pray at the right time is imperative, because it unlocks storerooms of miracles in God's Heavenly warehouse.

David gave the best time of his day to God (Psalm 55:17, 63:6). He sought Him early in the morning. There are practical benefits in seeking the Lord early or in the night hours; your mind is fresh, your body has rested and is more alert. In the night hours you can find more opportunity for quiet meditation on the Word of God. There is something in the quietness of the night and early morning that opens your ear to God's voice. Whenever you pray, the best time you give to the Lord is when it cost you the most.

King Solomon also made a practice of seeking the Lord early. He wrote that "he who seeks wisdom early will find him." He was talking about the Lord. Jesus is the wisdom of God (Proverbs 8:17), as the Prophet Isaiah also wrote.

"And the spirit of the LORD shall rest upon him, the spirit of wisdom and understanding, the spirit of counsel and might, the spirit of knowledge and of the fear of the LORD" (Isaiah 11:2, KJV).

"Saying with a loud voice, Worthy is the Lamb that was slain to receive power, and riches, and wisdom, and strength, and honor, and glory, and blessing" (Revelation 5:12, KJV).

Jesus was devoted to prayer and when we seek God in prayer we become more like His Son.

"Now in the morning, having risen a long while before daylight, He went out and departed to a solitary place; and there He prayed" (Mark 1:35).

He prayed throughout the night. "Now it came to pass in those days that He went out to the mountain to pray, and continued all night in prayer to God" (Luke 6:12).

We will have His nature because we are being transformed progressively into His likeness through a relationship of prayer.

Another important part of prayer involves God's timing. There is a time and a season for everything. In the New Testament Scriptures the Greek language has two different words for time, "chronos" and "kairos".

Chronos is the general time at which an event takes place, and kairos is used to signify a fixed time, definite season, or an opportune season.

Knowing the timing or "kairos" of God is praying specifically so God's power invades the natural realm in your situation to do something supernatural. David understood this in his relationship with God.

For instance, in one of David's stories in the first book of Samuel, we read that the Philistines attacked David and his people in Ziglag when they were at war. The Philistines took all the people in the town, including the children and females, captive... as well as their possessions. David was confused and spiritually low when he and his mighty men returned home. Some of his men were really upset to the extent that they had wanted to stone him.

"David was greatly distressed because the men were planning to stone him; each one of them was bitter in spirit because their sons and daughters had been captured, but David found strength in the LORD his God" (1 Samuel 30:6).

The story continues that King David encouraged himself, and asked the priest if he should pursue the enemy. God told him to pursue them for he would surely overtake and recover all that was forcefully taken from them. They did and recovered it all.

During the Old Testament, the priests were mediators between the people and God because the Lord Jesus had not yet come to earth as the Savior. This is the central reason why Jesus paid for our sins on the cross of Calvary. No longer is there the need for a mediator, a priest, or a go-between man and God.

We can therefore pray or talk to God directly. Even before the cross, David prayed directly to God through his songs. This was during critical times when he needed someone with a higher spiritual authority to intervene (1 Samuel 30: 6-7).

Through his prayers he was able to know the right timing to capture his enemies; recovering all the possessions the enemy had stolen. This was a "kairos" moment for David because his spirit was lifted up to hear, see, or sense divine direction from God. He would consult the Priest upon reminding himself of the Word of God.

Receiving direction from the Priest, he finally pursued his enemies and recovered all that had been stolen from the Israelites. "Kairos" played an important role in King David's survival as well as Jesus' survival. And if you are to survive in today's world, your greatest safety will come from a "kairos" prayer relationship with God.

King David escaped from the hands of King Saul's death threats when he sought refuge by the priests in the cave of Adullam. King Saul pursued David after he was informed of his whereabouts. Fortunately, David managed to escape, but unfortunately, the priests were murdered by King Saul.

David escaped from King Saul by hiding in this cave at Adullam. It was the right timing (kairos) for him to run away to safety (1 Samuel 22).

Your best direction and protection comes by prayer. It may not be a long prayer; it could be just few minutes. Your spiritual "antennae" must be sensitive to penetrate through all the waves and other interruptions in the spiritual realm to catch what God' Spirit is saying to you.

It was the prayers of Simeon who first discovered the revelation of the birth of the Messiah. Simeon was an old man in Jerusalem at the time the Lord Jesus was born.

"Now there was a man in Jerusalem called Simeon, who was righteous and devout. He was waiting for the consolation of Israel, and the Holy Spirit was on him. It had been revealed to him by the Holy Spirit that he would not die before he had seen the Lord's Messiah. Moved by the Spirit, he went into the temple courts. When his parents brought in the child Jesus to do for him what the custom of the Law required, Simeon took him up in his arms and praised God, saying:

"Sovereign Lord, as you have promised, you may now dismiss your servant in peace. For my eyes have seen your salvation, which you have prepared in the sight of all nations: a light for revelation to the Gentiles, and the glory of your people Israel."

"The child's father and mother marveled at what was said about him. Then Simeon blessed them and said to Mary, his mother: 'This child is destined to cause the falling and rising of many in Israel, and to be a sign that will be spoken against, so that the thoughts of many hearts will be revealed. And a sword will pierce your own soul too'" (Luke 2:22-35).

"Anna, who was always at the Temple praying and fasting, was able to discern when the Messiah would be born" (Luke 2:34-38). This kind of discernment is understood by those who pray and fast effectively. It takes a prayerful person to receive prophetic direction from God because the gift and the purpose of the prophetic word is to give one the enablement to hear from God.

However, the Holy Spirit who is the only Revelator will certainly give insight at times even though we may not be gifted prophetically. But it is necessary that we have a regular quiet time in His presence. The Muslims pray five times a day and if you have ever worked, lived or known devout Muslims, when it is time to pray, they stop everything and place their mats on the floor and pray consistently. How much more should our devotion be to Jesus?

Our prayer time could be in the morning, noon, evening or night. In the Jewish tradition, they have prayer times at 9 am, 12 pm and 3 pm. You have to set a time to meet with God, just as a married couple or friends set time to meet each other for a date.

Daily Discipline is Needed.

Prayer requires daily attention just like all other effective disciplines. A daily devotion to prayer is necessary for a strong relationship between you and God.

This means that your time with God must be consistently be a priority. Any good relationship between two people requires a consistent devotion to time with each other and there are many distractions in our world that competes for our attention.

But if we never become consistent in our prayer devotion with God, we will never get the benefits of experiencing Him, His favor and "winning the heart of God."

I learned from my previous Pastor, Dr. Bill Winston of Living Word Christian Center in Forest Park, IL how importance discipline is. I used to hear him telling the congregation that he sleeps early and wakes up at 3 am every day for his daily devotion. I started practicing that for over three years and gone back to sleeping late even though I'm an early person. I was being convicted as I stared writing on this topic so I'm going to be more diligent.

I think when the topic of discipline and devotion are being discussed, there was a special mother who left a legacy has to be acknowledged.

Mrs. Susannah Wesley, the mother of John and Charles Wesley, was an example of the power of consistent prayer. It was her prayers that saw her sons John became the founder of the Methodist Church and Charles became a great song writer and composer of the eighteenth century. She had birthed nineteen kids of whom ten survived. But her kids were never a deterrent to her prayer time. They would watch her flip her apron over her head to pray in the kitchen when she was distracted. She was a dedicated mother and wife and her life influenced and affected her children, especially John and Charles.

What distractions do you encounter in your daily life that robs your time with God?

Today's cell phone craze is very distractive, especially during the day. You can be on the phone for hours without accomplishing anything fruitful. Before there were cell phones, idle time in a waiting room usually meant reading a good book. But now we're flipping through the internet on our "smart phones." We are even giving more attention to cell phones than we are to television.

The most effective remedy is to disconnect our electronic distractions if possible when we are spending time with God. In biblical times they did not have to contend with telephones, television, the internet, and other technology. But there were other things that could have kept them distracted from following God.

There were many fears and rumors of wars that could have easily caused David to lose heart and quit believing God, but we see that though on several occasions he was worried or depressed, he encouraged himself and others through the Word of God and prayers.

Certainly King David was always communicating with God, because there were constant dangers that caused him to cry out to God. Some of his songs record how he woke up depressed or confused about his surroundings and when God would deliver him from his enemies. Yet he reminded himself of God's goodness and greatness and praised Him because he knew God was able to bring him out of every impossible situation.

The scriptures talk about the children of the tribe of Issachar; who "knew the times and seasons" (1 Chronicles 12:32). Knowing the "times and seasons" are necessary for prophetic prayer or prophetic intercession.

An example of prophetic prayer is for instance, if you need a reliable car but you don't have all the money for one, And as you pray you have the impression from the Holy Spirit to call forth the car and believe that you have it even though you have not seen it.

You take a step of faith and call forth a car to be released to you in Jesus' Name. That would be the right timing for God to open a door for the car to reach your end. Therefore miracle will eventually happen. Knowing the timing and calling it forth is a key. The prophetic can birth something into reality through faith which acts as a vehicle in bringing things that are unseen into manifestation.

Watching and Waiting is Necessary.

King David wrote "I waited patiently for the Lord; and he inclined unto me, and heard my cry. He brought me up also out of a horrible pit, out of the miry clay, and set my feet upon a rock" (Psalm 40:1-2).

God was training and equipping him to be the next King over Israel. He also trained his mighty men of war during that time. They were moving from one place to another seeking refuge for their souls. He experienced hunger and thirst (1 Samuel 21:6), but did not give up because he knew God was faithful to fulfill His promises.

He was not anxious to go ahead of the promises of God for his life. This means he watched and prayed, just as the Lord encourages you and I to watch and pray (Luke 21:36).

Being watchful and prayerful will position you to hear God's voice, know His plan and experience His power. It is very easy to miss His answer when you are not watchful. Therefore, we have to be watchful with the help of the Holy Spirit. "...the Spirit of Truth, has come, He will guide you into all truth; for He will not speak on

His own authority, but whatever He hears He will speak; and He will tell you things to come" (John 16:13).

Watching means to look or observe attentively, typical over a period of time.

Watching and waiting on the Lord is a discipline we all need. The watching and waiting does not mean that you are doing nothing except waiting on God to respond.

Watching and waiting on God is like someone waiting for a bus on a cold winter day. Waiting for a 30 minute arrival time can seem like several hours when you're waiting in the cold. But it also can seem like only several minutes.

It is the environment, mindset, condition or position you are in that will determine how the time passes, quickly or slowly. If you talk with someone while sitting there, the waiting time passes faster than expected, even though it may be bitterly cold.

When you are experiencing something productive, informative, or inspirational; your mindset plays a significant role in the waiting process. This is where a paradigm shift in your mindset helps you to enter into discovering God's will and laying down yours. Watching and waiting involves patience, but when you understand you have a role in the waiting, your mindset gives you the power to overcome impatience.

Each one of us is waiting on the Lord for something like King David wrote. It might be finances, the salvation of loved ones, the desire to marry, to have children, to be healthy, etc. Very seldom does it seem like answers from God come quickly.

That's why waiting on the Lord and believing in his word will help you to "Win the Heart of God." King David had to wait on God on different occasions and reasons, sometimes for years. He had so many enemies who were seeking to destroy his life. He waited for God to intervene instead of revenging himself. And this could be wearying. The best thing to do when you find yourself in a situation like King David found himself in, is to pray for grace to endure to the end. We even draw closer to God in such occasions like King David did by desiring to have an intimate relationship with God.

As you grow more intimate in your relationship with God, your trust for Him grows and brings you to the point of total surrender. He is able to do exceeding abundantly above all that you ask or even think according to the power that works in you (paraphrased, Ephesians 3:20).

The old Hymn by Louisa Stead from the nineteen century goes like this.

'Tis so sweet to trust in Jesus,

Just to take Him at His Word,

Just to rest upon His promise,

And to know "Thus saith the Lord"

Refrain.

Jesus, Jesus, how I trust Him!

How I've proved Him o'er and o'er;

Jesus, Jesus, precious Jesus! Oh, for grace to trust Him more.

King David learned how to wait on the Lord through his songs. God needed to form a kingly character in him before enthroning him as a King over Israel. It took a long time for David to become King after he was anointed by the Prophet Samuel. Often times you may face a long wait before you see answers to prayer. The book of Isaiah also shows us how important it is to learn how to pray and wait on the Lord.

"Even the youth shall faint and be weary, and the young men shall utterly fall, but they that wait upon the Lord shall renew their strength; they shall mount up with wings as eagles; they shall run and not be weary, and they shall walk and not faint" (Isaiah 40:30-31, KJV).

Waiting time is not wasted time when you're waiting on the Lord. Instead it is a mechanism to shape us to be people characterized by the nature of God. Learning to wait on the Lord brings about spiritual maturity.

Faith is another important ingredient in the power of prayer. David was a man of faith according to the book of Hebrews (Hebrews 11:32). Our faith also plays a big role in waiting on God. The scriptures teaches us that without faith it is impossible to please God (Hebrews 11:6), and the Apostle John also wrote, "for whatsoever is born of God overcometh the world even our faith" (1 John 5:4).

We grow in our faith like Abraham. Abraham who had faith in God was called the father of faith because he obeyed and believed

God for His promises, though in the natural sense those promises were impossible.

Abraham was a man of prayer. He always communicated with God and built altars for God yet, He failed God by accepting Sarah's offer to have children through her maid servant, Hagar. Because of fear, on two occasions he lied that Sarah was his sister (Genesis 12: 11-20, 20:2). However in the end he was credited for righteous because he had faith in God for the impossible. This is why "it was credited to him as righteousness" (Romans 4:22).

Jesus also rebuked His disciples and the Jews about their lack of faith. (Mark 16:14, Matthew 8:23-27)

The Old Testament saints backed up their faith with sacrifices they placed on the altar. David built an altar for God for a peace sacrifice (2 Samuel 24-25).

An altar is a place of worship, a place where you sacrifice your life to the Lord. It is a place of exchange. This means that David was sold out completely to God. You place your gifts on the altar and offer them as a sacrifice to God. This is a sign to you and God that you put your full trust or faith in Him.

A Fervent Prayer

Prayer has always been the nucleus of most religious faiths and Christianity is no exception. We know prayer is very important.

However, what is "fervent prayer?"

Well, almost everyone prays and everyone's hoping for answers. However, fervent prayer or the "effective prayer of the righteous" requires such disciplines as "watching and praying," patience, and waiting on God. This tests our faith and that of others. We can find many examples of heroes in the Bible who were champions of fervent prayer.

James the Apostle, the Lord Jesus' half-brother wrote about the effective prayer of the righteous. He talked about the Prophet Elijah (James 5:17).

"Elijah was a regular human being with feelings, affections, and a constitution like ours: and he prayed earnestly for it not to rain, and no rain fell on the earth for three years and six months (1Kings17:1) and then he prayed again and the heavens supplied rain, and the land produced its crops as usual" (1Kings18:42-45, Amp).

All the heroes of faith in the eleventh chapter of the book of Hebrews had weaknesses or failures; however they were patient and held fast to their faith and waited for God's promises through fervent prayer.

Watch and Pray

Learning to wait on God after praying is necessary. What do we mean by "learning to wait on God?"

Often you abandon your prayers because the answer doesn't come quickly enough. When you are no longer in anticipation of getting an answer or the expected results, you know that you are no longer waiting!

Sometimes you may get busy or you need to rush to get your daily chores done, hence it can make it more difficult to hear from God. It requires discipline to wait on the Lord with fervent prayer.

Like me, you may have prayed for hours but have never taken the time to wait and listen to God; how God would respond because your mind would already be looking forward to something else.

A good practical discipline to use when you are praying is to maintain a journal and record your talks with God.

What you say to Him, what He says to you, and how you are to follow through with the results. You can always journal in a notebook or you might have a recorder of some sort. If you hear from God in the middle of traffic, a recorder can be of great use.

The Lord told the disciples to watch and pray that they may not enter into temptation (paraphrased, Matthew 26:41).

You may think you have good prayers, but if you are not watchful, you will miss your answer and God's perfect plan for the situation. Waiting on the Lord is a discipline that grows progressively as we learn to hear God's voice by waiting patiently. Patience has always had negative overtones. But it is a discipline that helps to make sense of your circumstances.

David was able to wait patiently for the Lord because he purposed it in his mind. Patience is a fruit of the spirit that teaches you the timing of God's answer. Exactly when an answer comes through is not as important as how it comes through (Galatians 5:22-23).

You need to practice walking and living in the spirit like a toddler learns how to walk. It is step by step, when we purpose our mind to do so. However, the most important thing is allowing the Holy Spirit to possess you because only He can teach and guide you to the expected end.

When King David was pursued by King Saul, he waited patiently for God to avenge on his behalf. He even had the chance to kill Saul. Even though David's rights were violated, he was able to wait on the Lord until the end of the trial and God promoted him.

You probably have gone to your parents looking for an answer and yet they are silent. God, our Heavenly Parent also is silent at times. In some cases that silence is the answer in itself. During those long periods of silence and waiting on the Lord, God takes the opportunity to develop our character as we wait on him patiently.

Many times when you present your fervent prayer before God it doesn't seem like he is answering.

There are times when spiritual strongholds need to be broken or we have wrong motives as the Apostle James wrote "Or you do ask God for them, and yet fail to receive because you ask with wrong motives. Your intention is when you get what you desire to spend it in sensual pleasures" (James 4:3, Amp).

Strongholds are the powers of darkness or evil spirits that try to withhold the answers to our prayers and fight against every good thing that you purpose your mind and heart to do. In such cases only the Spirit of God can reveal them to us and we have to pull them down and destroy them so that we can have our answers from God.

The discipline of waiting on the Lord for your prayer request will often take longer than you expected which can be frustrating. But whatever it takes to put your trust in God's timing, it will be important for the answer to your prayer and the development of godly character is a part of God's blessing.

The Apostle Paul wrote it clearly to the believers in Rome, and certainly for us all: "Moreover let us exult and triumph in our troubles and rejoice in our sufferings knowing that pressure and affliction and hardship; patience and unswerving endurance; Fortitude develops maturity of character, approved faith, and tried integrity.

And character of this sort produces the habit of a joyful and the confident hope of eternal salvation. Such hope never disappoints, deludes or shames us, for God's love has been poured out in our hearts through the Holy Spirit who has been given to us (Romans 5:1-5, Amp).

God gives us supernatural strength to wait on him when we pray. King David's life shows us great examples.

David's prayer life preserved him until he received answers from God. He just trusted in God's Word that He is not like a man who would lie. The testimonies of his forefathers coupled with what God had done for him personally were enough to believe the Word of God.

You often think of your testimony as how you accepted the Lord as Savior. But your testimony is more than that. It is every word you speak. The words that come out of your mouth are your testimonies. The testimony of your words is very powerful.

Someone else's testimony can stretch your faith as well. When you hear the testimony of how the power of God changes someone's life, it gives you power to expect the same for yourself.

We overcome the devil by our testimonies. "They overcame the enemy by the Blood of the Lamb and the Word of their testimony" (Revelation 12:11).

The subject of fervent prayer is usually focused around God and you. However, there is often a third player in the success of your prayers. There are times we can go to pastors, leaders or friends in the Church to support you in prayer.

With a little wisdom and allowing the Holy Spirit to lead you to the right people at the right time; prayer support from others can increase the power of prayer in your life.

It may be risky to reach out to others at times, but with guidance from the Holy Spirit, sharing your heart with those you can trust increases the power of God in your life.

There will always be counselors available to you, friends and family with more wisdom or experience that can help you power-up your prayer life and get answers.

Another important thing is to remember that David experienced many failures in his life. His faith was tested in various ways. All the great heroes of our faith were tested and they all failed at one point, yet God saw them righteous.

For example; Abraham lied (Genesis 20), Isaac lied (Genesis 26), Moses murdered an Egyptian (Exodus 2) and Samson fell for a prostitute (Judges 16). However, when God forgives, failure is not the final verdict, so no matter how you fall you can get up and stand again.

Another vital ingredient to fervent prayer is love. Love is like the curtain rod that holds up the entire curtain. Without it, faith, hope, and even prayer have nothing to hang on. You might pray for hours, but without love it is all fruitless.. Love for God motivates us to wait on Him. Love is a discipline which necessitates a fervent prayer.

The affection that you have to marry someone will cause you to wait for that person even if it is for a long time. Jacob was a great example of a man who served and waited for fourteen years for the woman he loved. You can do a study on his life to learn more about waiting on the Lord (Genesis 29).

This brings us to the question; should our prayers be long or short? Well, we read how the Prophet Elijah confronted the prophets of Baal (1 Kings 18:25-40). His prayers were very short but God showed up!

Yet we may also find that these men of old, and even the Lord, would spend hours before God in prayer before appearing in public. You could compare it to an athlete who shows up for game day, but he has been on the practice field many hours with the vision of becoming a champion.

It is not recorded whether David prayed before he fought with Goliath. Perhaps he prayed quietly within himself as he watched Goliath rushing at him. Perhaps he heard the voice of God before he killed Goliath. But one thing is for sure, it was against all odds.

David's life of prayer and devotion to God had God's power in it. We read about Nehemiah, Daniel, Jeremiah, Ezra and many other servants of God who prayed to Him concerning their life issues. Hopeless or impossible situations by God's people were solved through prayer. Some just spoke the word with faith with only a few words and God showed up. Your prayers can be lengthy or short depending on the situation or your passion for God and His power. With great passion David found himself in the presence of God praying for long hours but the most important thing is that he was being led by the Holy Spirit and God demonstrated His power.

Below are some Points for Prayer

When do we Pray? - We can pray at all times and when we study the Bible, we see that Jesus often prayed early in the morning (Mark1:35) or at night, sometimes throughout the night (Luke 6:12-13).

Prayer must be constant and we must pray without ceasing. (1 Thessalonians 5:17).

Prayer is no different than breathing. It is something you will do constantly because it will keep you alive.

A soldier will not go into battle without his weapon. You simply cannot refuse to pray because you don't know how. There is not a specific formula for praying. As you develop your habits in prayer the Holy Spirit will help you. The following is a popular prayer guide acronym called A.C.T.S (just like the book of Acts).

A– Adoration

C- Confession

T-Thanksgiving

S- Supplication

These were taken from the book of Philippians (4:4-7).

It is just a guideline of prayer. "Rejoice in the Lord always. Again I will say, rejoice"! "Let your gentleness be known to all men. The Lord *is* at hand. Be anxious for nothing, but in everything by prayer and supplication, with thanksgiving, let your requests be made known to God; and the peace of God, which surpasses all understanding, will guard your hearts and minds through Christ Jesus."

Adoration is praising God, magnifying His Name, making His Name "Big" (Colossian3:16).

Confession is telling God your sins, your family's sins, and even the sins of your ancestors. The sins of your family and ancestors can affect your life indirectly. Even the sins of your city, nation and leaders can affect you indirectly. For example Lot's household was influenced by the sins of the people of Sodom and Gomorrah (Genesis 19).

God has established prayer for you to ask for forgiveness and cleansing We must come to God with a repentant heart and confess our sins.

"If we confess our sins, He is faithful and just to forgive us *our* sins and to cleanse us from all unrighteousness" (1John1:8-9).

Thanksgiving is your thankfulness to God for yourself, your loved ones, community, nation and your future, (1Thessalonians 5:18), "in everything give thanks; for this is the will of God in Christ Jesus for you."

Supplication is your petitions, requests, or intercession for others (praying on behalf of someone else). It is always good to pray for all of your community, family, friends, neighbors, the government, your President, Prime Minister, Queens etc.

Praying for others teaches us to live as Jesus lived, focusing outward towards others instead of being focused inward.

You can make a roster; Monday through Sunday with your prayer list on it. You will experience a change in your prayer and personal life as you start praying for other because God honors that(1 Timothy 2:1-5).

Important Keys to an Effective Prayer

Probably the first thing one must think of for effective prayer is whether there is any lack of forgiveness in your heart. The Scriptures make it clear that if you do not forgive those who have sinned against you, God will not forgive you (Matthew 6:14). This verse is right after the Lord's Prayer. And also the Lord spoke about the prayer of faith and said

"Therefore I tell you, whatever you ask for in prayer, believe that you have received it, and it will be yours. And when you stand praying, if you hold anything against anyone, forgive them, so that your Father in heaven may forgive you your sins" (Mark 11:24-25).

Our prayers can be hindered because of un-forgiveness. King David had a forgiving heart or else he would have killed King Saul and many of the Israelites who hated him.

• Let the Holy Spirit guide you. "However, when He, the Spirit of truth, has come, He will guide you into all truth; for He will not speak of His own *authority,* but whatever He hears He will speak; and He will tell you things to come" (John 16:13).

• Pray in the Spirit (Ephesians 6:18). This builds your faith, and empowers you with holy boldness to speak. When we pray in the spirit, our spirits communicate with God directly (1 Corinthian 14: 2, Jude1:20, Acts 4:31).

• Pray in faith. Confess *your* trespasses to one another, and pray for one another, that you may be healed. The effective, fervent prayer of a righteous man avails much (James 5:14-16).

• Pray to God in Jesus' Name (John14:14). The Lord Jesus said that no one comes to the Father except through Him (John: 14-6). Gods' Name shows His Character and what He does. The Jews called Him YHWH- no vowel (English-Yahweh), which means LORD.

Some of His names are. Yahweh Jireh, meaning the LORD will provide, Yahweh Nissi, meaning The LORD is my Banner, Yahweh Shalom meaning the LORD is peace, Yahweh Tsidkenu meaning the Lord our righteousness, etc.

The Lord Jesus also has the same Attributes and Characteristics. We pray in His Name, or go to the Father through Him; that is an order of protocol. Our Lord Jesus said He and the Father are one.

• Believe to get answers from God (Mark 11:22-25).

• We must pray the will of God (Matthew 6:10). Our will must be in alignment with His will.

The Apostle John wrote "And this is the confidence (the assurance, the privilege of boldness) which we have in Him (we are sure) that if we ask anything (make any request) according to His will (in agreement with His own plan) He listens to us and hears us, and if (since) we (positively) know that He listens to us and hears us in whatever we ask, we also know (with settled and absolute knowledge that we have (granted us as our present possession) the requests made in Him" (1John 5:14-15, Amp).

• Use God's Word to pray back to God what He has said and promised He would do until you get results. This is called praying the Word (Acts 4:24).

• Before exercising the discipline of prayer, allow a time of quietness, reflection and meditation so the Holy Spirit has an opportunity to direct your thoughts. The Spirit will often provide you Scripture that matches your situation or problem.

• Set a time to pray (quiet time) to avoid distractions. It is better if you set your alarm at least thirty minutes earlier than your normal wake-up time to start an early morning discipline of prayer. Wash your face to keep you awake and read the Scriptures and worship. If early morning hours are not the best times for you because of your work schedule and family commitment, you can still set a time to have an intimacy with the Lord.

Use the book of Psalms to sing your own melody to God, which is called a new song. Just start praising Him for even waking you up as the Holy Spirit helps you to start your day. He will take control and guide you.

After your initial prayer of thanksgiving, wait a few minutes in His presence, listen for God to speak to you; it could be a phrase, a sentence, a song, or verse in the Bible; whichever way God chooses to speak. We must compare what we hear with the Word of God, especially in times of making critical decisions.

Use a journal to keep dates and records of what God speaks to you. It is important to always thank God and also share testimonies on answered prayers. Testimonies bring encouragement to your faith. It will also deposit contagious faith in whoever you share them with.

Praying together as a family opens the way for us to teach our kids how to pray which is necessary because we are preparing the next generation. They will be strong to face any problem in our absence. They will not panic, but trust in the Word of God sown into them.

You can compare it to a reservoir holding tons of water that we draw from during the draught season. Every household that prays together stays together. Couples must pray together, parents and children must pray together. It is good for the entire family to pray together several times a month.

In years past, as a youth teacher, I've asked the students why is it that they can talk on their cell phones for hours with their friends, but whenever it was time to pray they can only pray for a few minutes and stop. One of them said "Teacher, when I talk to my friend she talks back, both of us are engaged in the conversation, but when I talk to God, I do all the talking, He does not respond so I get bored."

Is that your story too?

But God does talk back to us. The Holy Spirit is always talking to you. The problem is in our listening. The routines of life usually keep us from hearing. We can also have our plans already decided, and we take the initiative to go forward without hearing from God.

The devil knows the power of prayer. That's why he has worked through people over the past years to abolish prayer at schools and certain public sectors. In some nations like Ghana, where I am familiar with, they still pray at the schools. It doesn't completely stop chaos in the schools, but it limits Satan from taking more control, like we see in America and in some parts of the world.

What happened after prayer was taken out of schools? The devil certainly took over. It is not only in schools that we have kicked God out. When light departs, darkness comes in automatically. Should it be any surprise that we see guns everywhere, even among kids in schools and colleges in America? It is not too late for God to restore all those in the U.S. through the travailing prayer of faithful believers.

The fervent prayer of the righteous is effective and powerful. King David did not have any concordance, no study Bible, no resources besides the Torah. He was able to pray fervently and captured God's heart. Our effective prayers can definitely reverse all the negative plots of the devil.

I believe with all my heart there is going to be a shift and shaking in the United States and all across the globe for the preparation of the Bride of Christ for the end-time harvest. EVERY PRAYER MATTERS (EPM). Through your prayers you can be a man or woman after God's own heart!

May God cause an entire generation to rise up that will re-dig the old well of prayers; people that will pray fervently for His Kingdom to come on earth as it is in Heaven. People like Charles Finney, Smith Wigglesworth, Andrew Murray, Jonathan Edwards, George Mueller, etc.

The prayers of the righteous should never be under estimated. There is power in prayer, hence we should pray and not faint. God wants to answer your prayers! Therefore pray without ceasing.

The fervent prayer of the righteous avails much. Never give up in talking to God or asking Him. God is obligated to answer the prayer of the righteous. He said call and I will answer. He does answer the prayer of the sinner of out His love and mercy. At the same time we have to know His will for our life when we ask.

Continuous prayers prepare us to face the giants in every area of our life. Prayer is like a savings account where one deposits money and withdraw when the need arises.

Like David, look at the greatness of God rather than the circumstances you are facing. The more we look to God the smaller the problem would become!

Personal Notes.

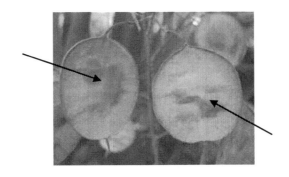

The arrows show the translucent parts of the honesty flower.

Chapter 4

A Man of Integrity- Honesty is the Best Policy

Honesty and "doing what you say" has always been a trademark of a good character . It is interesting that the "honesty flower" from South Eastern Europe has coin-shaped seedpods that are translucent. That's why the flower's namesake represents transparency and integrity.

An honest person is transparent. There shouldn't be an extreme difference between actions at home compared to actions in public. However, depending on our environment and circumstances, we all behave differently to some degree.

What is it that makes us act differently when we're on the job or when we're at Church? It's like having a dual personality but instead of freedom it produces stress. When we try to present ourselves differently than we truly are, it hurts our character more than the people we are trying to deceive. It always costs to be honest but it is worth it.

Several Scriptures describe King David as an honest man of integrity, in spite of the testimonies of his sin. In addition to declaring his integrity, David was also bold enough to ask God to "search his heart and know his thoughts." It takes courage to tell God to search your heart if you know you're not living right before Him.

"Search me, O God, and know my heart;
Try me, and know my anxieties;
And see if there *is any* wicked way in me,
And lead me in the way everlasting" (Psalm 139:23-24).

God knew that David was a man of integrity even before he was anointed as King over Israel. Integrity is a characteristic of God and He wants His children to be people of integrity.

The moral standard of today's society has become corrupt in almost every sector that you can imagine. But God knows your heart and if you are a person of your word. No one is perfect, but without honesty who could be trusted? You may sin, but do you keep it real?

According to the book of Psalms, God knew David's failures but also considered him a man of integrity who kept his word and moreover was a trusted leader.

"He chose David as his servant and took him from the sheepfolds: From following the ewes great with young He brought him to feed Jacob his people, and Israel his inheritance. So he fed them according to the integrity of his heart; and guided them by the skillfulness of his hands" (Psalms 76:70-72).

King David wrote in one of his psalms that he had walked in integrity (Psalm 26).

"Vindicate me, O Lord, for I have walked in my integrity; I have [expectantly] trusted in, leaned on, *and* relied on the Lord without wavering *and* I shall not slide.

"Examine me, O Lord, and prove me; test my heart and my mind. "For Your loving-kindness is before my eyes, and I have walked in Your truth [faithfully]. I do not sit with false persons, nor fellowship with pretenders; "I hate the company of evildoers and will not sit with the wicked.

"I will wash my hands in innocence, and go about Your altar, O Lord, "That I may make the voice of thanksgiving heard and may tell of all Your wondrous works.

"Lord, I love the habitation of Your house, and the place where Your glory dwells. "Gather me not with sinners *and* sweep me not away [with them], nor my life with bloodthirsty men,

"In whose hands is wickedness, and their right hands are full of bribes. "But as for me, I will walk in my integrity; redeem me and be merciful *and* gracious to me. "My foot stands on an even place; in the congregations will I bless the Lord."

His feet standing on an even place means that his life is consistent. The previous Scripture passages are not the only proof of his integrity and honesty. King David had many followers who knew that he would be anointed King. He demonstrated good character to his followers and many were ready to sacrifice their life for him. David was very caring toward his people because as their leader he knew he was accountable to God for all the people under his jurisdiction.

Character and Integrity.

Character is formed by repeatedly making the same choices. When you teach your child to respect adults and he practices it over and over it becomes part of him.

However, integrity is a character trait that goes deeper. It comes from an individual's heart and cannot be polluted, compromised or imitated. A character trait may come automatically but integrity has to be learned.

If a man has integrity and he sees a character flaw, he will work on eliminating that undesirable flaw from his life. Leaders have to be people of character and most of all integrity. Sometimes we follow leaders who are eloquent in speech and attractive, but integrity makes a good leader.

King David was a true leader who set a good example for his followers. His men of valor were well-trained and ready to follow orders because he was trustworthy.

We have seen and heard false leaders of nations and Churches in this century that have deceived many. Some have claimed to be the Christ. Many are genuinely looking for the truth but unfortunately fall into deception. Then there are those who know they are deceived and doomed but they don't care about the consequences.

Some are loyal and ready to die for their leaders, like King David's warriors. However, some follow in ignorance.

For example, most people heard of David Koresh of Waco, Texas who died with his followers in April 1993. He was a cult leader and deceived his followers into believing he was a prophet. A self-professed Christ. Jim Jones was also a cult leader who deceived many people. They flew to Guyana from the U.S and he caused his followers to commit suicide because the world was coming to an end. We see more of such stories around the world.

This reminds me of Dr. Kofi Annan who was a United Nations special envoy to Syria in 2011-2012. He was frustrated over the war in Syria, and also that world leaders were not cooperating. He was interviewed concerning the civil war and the position he was vacating when presenting his resignation on August 31st 2012. He said, "The world is full of crazy people like me, so don't be surprised if someone else decides to take it." Right! Some people are busy-bodies just looking for something to do.

King David was purpose- driven until he lost focus. He was a warrior and when he took his focus off the battlefield that was when he got in trouble.

God said in His Word that He does not break His covenant and people of integrity are expected to keep their covenants (Psalm 89:34).

David kept his covenant with King Saul's son, Jonathan; even after Jonathan died (2 Samuel 9). David and Jonathan had a covenant to protect each other. Jonathan knew that his father wanted to kill David because of jealousy and insecurity. He therefore aided David to escape from Saul's palace. King Saul was very angry at Jonathan because he suspected Jonathan knew David's whereabouts.

Jonathan knew and confessed to David that he knew his father's reign as King over Israel would certainly come to an end soon and made the way for David to become the next King.

David agreed that he would remember Jonathan when he becomes a King. David therefore brought Jonathan's son Mephibosheth to the palace and cared for him (1 Samuel 20).

When King David began to reign over Israel, he inquired if there was someone in King Saul's house that he might show kindness to because of Jonathan. He learned that Jonathan's son Mephibosheth was living in a city called Lo-Debar. Mephibosheth was crippled from an accident. His nurse dropped him when he was about five years old. When the news came that King Saul and his son Jonathan had died, Mephibosheth's nurse was trying to get him out of the palace quickly when she accidentally dropped him (2 Samuel 4:4).

King David ordered that an allotment of land be given to Mephibosheth and he was to eat at the King's table which meant he was reinstated as a royalty because of David's integrity. My prayer is that the favor of God would come upon you now as you read this book and may God restore all that the devil has stolen from you. May the restoration start today!

King David could have completely forgotten Jonathan after he and his father Saul died in battle. Even subsequent turmoil in King Saul's household that resulted in the death of several more of his children did not deter King David from keeping his word.

King David longed for the presence of God and he knew he had to be a man of integrity. He was afraid of living a life without God.

Have you ever done something wrong and soon felt the absence of the Holy Spirit in you? King David experienced that after he committed adultery with Bathsheba.

He truly repented of his sins because he was very transparent and honest! He wrote about the Holy Spirit in his penitential song, pleading with God not to take His Holy Spirit from him (Psalms 51:11). This means he knew the important role of the Holy Spirit in his life. You are spiritually dead without the Holy Spirit and if you have lived in the presence of God for a long time, you do not want to yield to temptation and exchange it for anything less.

Someone said if the devil offers you something for sale and you refuse to buy it, he will offer it to you free, so watch out! The Devil is crafty and he always wants to trap people into sin, death and destruction. We therefore have to walk in the spirit and in the Word of God so that we will not gratify the desires of our flesh. (Galatians 5:16).

I believe when we associate with people of integrity their life should definitely affect and challenge us to live right.

The Scripture talks about certain individuals that were people of integrity in both the Old and the New Testament. Daniel was a man of integrity who made a difference in the life of others. He was a young Prophet who was carried into exile in 605 B.C by the Babylonians. He wrote the book of Daniel in the Old Testament.

His life influenced and impacted other young men in the Bible like Shadrach, Meshach and Abednego (Daniel 3). They were thrown in a furnace of fire because they would not bow down or compromise to an idol. They upheld their integrity. Joseph, the son of Jacob was a young man who had the character of God. He was honest and the Scripture describes him as a man of integrity (Genesis 39:8-15). His brothers sold him into slavery because of their jealousy. Even though they meant to do him evil, God turned it for good.

He was a slave in Potiphar's house; he did not want to sin against God or man. His master Potiphar was one of King Pharaoh's captains. When his wife wanted to rape Joseph, he ran away leaving his coat in the hands of Potiphar's wife. She reported Joseph to her husband who threw Joseph into prison. Joseph was not bitter at her or his master and he loved and forgave his brothers who sold him to slavery. God reconciled him to his brothers and later his entire family (Genesis 45:1-15).

Joseph, the earthly father of the Lord Jesus was also a man of integrity. The gospel of Matthew records his plan to separate quietly from Mary when he saw that she was pregnant though they were not married (Matthew 1:19).

It is very easy to compromise the truth in this perverted generation, however; lies cannot be hidden forever. Lies are uncovered when the light exposes the darkness. People compromise because of power, pleasures of the world. We do not compromise when we are filled and led by the Sprit of God.

Integrity is a characteristic all believers should pursue. It is difficult to grow spiritually without integrity. No one is perfect, but we have to strive to grow spiritually.

There are certain things God will not reveal to spiritual infants. You must therefore grow spiritually if you desire spiritual revelation from God. "Now I say *that* the heir, as long as he is a child, does not differ at all from a slave, though he is master of all, but is under guardians and stewards until the time appointed by the father"(Galatians 4:1-2).

David always maintained his integrity in doing good. He remained loyal and faithful to King Saul after he slew Goliath and the women were singing "Saul has slain his thousand and David has slain ten thousand." Even when King Saul wanted to kill him he never sought revenge.

We can also learn from the book of Proverbs from King Solomon who wrote the advice he learned from his father David. David told him to shun evil counsel. King Solomon wrote how his father prepared him to fulfill his destiny.

"When I [Solomon] was a son with my father [David], tender and the only son in the sight of my mother [Bathsheba],

"He taught me and said to me, let your heart hold fast my words; keep my commandments and live.

"Get skillful *and* godly Wisdom, get understanding (discernment, comprehension, and interpretation); do not forget and do not turn back from the words of my mouth.

"Forsake not [Wisdom], and she will keep, defend, *and* protect you; love her, and she will guard you.

"The beginning of Wisdom is: get Wisdom (skillful and godly Wisdom)! [For skillful *and* godly Wisdom is the principal thing.]

And with all you have gotten, get understanding (discernment, comprehension, and interpretation).

"Prize Wisdom highly *and* exalt her, and she will
exalt *and* promote you; she will bring you to honor when you
embrace her.

"She shall give to your head a wreath of gracefulness; a crown of beauty *and* glory will she delivers to you.

"Hear, O my son, and receive my sayings, and the years of your life shall be many.

"I have taught you in the way of skillful *and* godly Wisdom [which is comprehensive insight into the ways and purposes of God]; I have led you in paths of uprightness.

"When you walk, your steps shall not be hampered [your path will be clear and open]; and when you run, you shall not stumble.

"Take firm hold of instruction, do not let go; guard her, for she is your life.

"Enter not into the path of the wicked, and go not in the way of evil men.

"Avoid it, do not go on it; turn from it and pass on.

"For they cannot sleep unless they have caused
trouble *or* vexation; their sleep is taken away unless they have
caused someone to fall.

"For they eat the bread of wickedness and drink the wine of violence.

"But the path of the [uncompromisingly] just *and* righteous is like the light of dawn, that shines more and more (brighter and clearer) until [it reaches its full strength and glory in] the perfect day [to be prepare

"The way of the wicked is like deep darkness; they do not know over what they stumble.

"My son, attend to my words; consent *and* submit to my sayings.

"Let them not depart from your sight; keep them in the center of your heart.

"For they are life to those who find them, healing *and* health to all their flesh.

"Keep *and* guard your heart with all vigilance *and* above all that you guard, for out of it flow the springs of life

"Put away from you false and dishonest speech, and willful *and* contrary talk put far from you.

"Let your eyes look right on [with fixed purpose], and let your gaze be straight before you.

"Consider well the path of your feet, and let all your ways be established *and* ordered aright.

"Turn not aside to the right hand or to the left; remove your foot from evil" (Proverbs 4).

King David was the only King in Israel's history who prepared his son for kingship. From these Scriptures we read about the seeds planted in young King Solomon that were fruitful as an adult. It wasn't a surprise that he asked God for discernment when God asked him what he wanted.

King David's heart for his son Solomon was to reverence God and avoid the mistakes he made. However, despite David's warnings, Solomon strayed, opened the door to idolatry, ruined his reign and lost many blessings from God.

Among all the names of people of integrity mentioned in the Bible, none of them were known as the man after God's own heart except King David.

Personal Notes
Integrity is priceless yet it costs to live a life of honesty

GOD	MAN
1: Do not worship any other gods 2: Do not make any idols 3: Do not misuse the name of God 4: Keep the Sabbath holy	5: Honour your father & mother 6: Do not murder 7: Do not commit adultery 8: Do not steal 9: Do not lie 10: Do not covet

The Word of God is infallible. The Word of God is Life!

Chapter 5

Knowing The Word of God- Knowing God!

God's Word is powerful. It can be categorized in two. The written word, or the Scriptures that we read... and the Rhema word, or spoken Word of God. The spoken or Rhema Word is when someone is reading the Scriptures or listening to the Word of God and an insight or revelation comes into the mind or spirit of that person about the Word of God relating to that individual's situation or that which would be a direction, a word of encouragement, correction etc. By the application of a revelation dreams could be fulfilled. Being only a listener without also being a doer, amounts to unfulfilled dreams.

For instance, the Prophet Daniel was one of the captives from Judah to the land of Persia and he read the prophecy of Jeremiah that said God would restore Jerusalem after a period of seventy years.

111

When he read that his spirit was quickened and he went before the Lord with prayer, fasting and sackcloth (mourning cloth). Because the set time was due for the captives to return to Jerusalem (Daniel 9:2, Jeremiah 25:12).

God answered his prayers because he acted on the spoken word he had read in the written word of God.

According to the Jewish tradition, the Jews were supposed to teach their children the word of God from their infancy. "And you must commit yourselves wholeheartedly to these commands that I am giving you today. Repeat them again and again to your children. Talk about them when you are at home and when you are on the road, when you are going to bed and when you are getting up" (Deuteronomy 6:6-7, NLT).

One can therefore conclude that it was a command from God for the Jews to know and believe in the Word of God and pass it on to their children as a heritage and then to the next generation as long as the generations continued to exist.

The Jews are particular about the inspired Word of God. The Bible was written in Hebrew, then Aramaic (language spoken by the Semitic family) then Greek.

The Bible means "The Books" from the Greek word "ta biblia." Therefore the Holy Bible is simply "The Holy Books."

Of course, the Jews are very particular about the Torah and the prophetic books written by the Prophets. The prophetic books from Isaiah through Malachi were written centuries after the death of King David.

The Torah is the first five books of the Bible which were written by Moses. They consist of the account of creation through the exodus of the Israelites (from Egypt), of God giving the laws and the Ten Commandments to Moses on Mount Sinai and of the journey through the wilderness.

Therefore the written Word of God was nothing new to King David, since he had to bind them on his neck so he could read them when he went out and came in the house. You could say the Word was like bread, water, air and life to the Jews.

King David wasn't like some folks who just have a "head knowledge" of God's Word and lack a real revelation of it. Like the Pharisee, scribes etc as the Lord would question them of their faith and so forth. He used the Word of God as a measuring stick for them.

The word of God is the "manual" for all who profess Christ as Lord and Savior.

The Word guides us, giving us direction, encouragement, instruction, wisdom, protection, satisfaction, salvation, and restoration... in short there is "hope" in the Word of God. God said His people perish because of a lack of knowledge (Hosea 4: 6).

It is said that ignorance of the law is no excuse. When you park at a place with 'NO PARKING" sign and you get a ticket from the Police, the judge is not going to waive the fine with the excuse that you didn't see it. Because they expect everyone to obey the law. You are responsible therefore for whatever you do.

The Lord Jesus showed the believers how to use the Word of God as a weapon to defeat the devil. He was tempted by Satan after He had fasted forty days and nights.

He told Satan "It is written." What is written is written. The devil knows those who do not know or walk in the Word of God and he is not afraid of them.

The more we know the Word of God the more we know God. There is a difference between knowing the Word of God and believing it.

Knowing merely goes with the mind,(head knowledge) while believing goes with the heart. Some people know the scriptures by memory but they do not believe it so the Word is not beneficial to them.

This was not so with King David. He was a student of the Word and believed in it. He was the most famous King in the history of Israel.

Even though his son King Solomon was the richest and wisest person in history, King David had and still has a good reputation and honor by the Jews because of his relationship with God and of his accomplishments than was his son Solomon.

David knew the Word of God and because he had a reverential fear for God he tried to walk in the Word. That also gave him the advantage of writing the songs in the book of Psalms.

King David had the gift of encouragement. He was able to encourage himself in the Lord (Word of God) even when no one was on his side (1 Samuel 30:6). He wrote:

The law of the LORD *is* perfect, converting the soul;
The testimony of the LORD *is* sure, making wise the simple;
The statutes of the LORD *are* right, rejoicing the heart; The commandment of the LORD *is* pure, ...

Yea, than much fine gold;
Sweeter also than honey and the honeycomb.
 Moreover by them Your servant is warned,
And in keeping them *there is* great reward" (Psalm 19:8-11).

He understood and realized that the Word of God is pure. Both the written and spoken Word are true because God cannot lie.

He compared the sweetness of the Word of God to honey. He said it is sweeter than honey. Do you believe that? Sometimes you may be spiritually dry and someone may give you a Word of God or encouragement that could revive your spirit. There is nothing that can bring nourishment to your soul than the Word of God.

He believed that the Word of God warns every child of God, so in reality it protects us.   He wrote several Psalms about God's protection because King Saul and a couple of people including his own son made him a fugitive.

The LORD is my rock, my fortress, and my savior; my God is my rock, in whom I find protection. He is my shield, the power that saves me, and my place of safety (Psalm 18:2).

The Word of God preserves and guides our lives. The Psalmist wrote.

"How can a young man cleanse his way?
By taking heed according to Your word.
With my whole heart I have sought You;
Oh, let me not wander from Your commandments!
Your word I have hidden in my heart,
That I might not sin against You." (Psalm 119:9-11).

Have you hidden the Word of God within you? If not, what are you waiting for? The more we hide the Word of God in our heart the less and lesser sins we would commit. Even as we pray the Lord's Prayer and we ask God to deliver us from temptation. Temptations are inevitable therefore if you resist temptation you resist Satan and you win.

King David said there is a reward for those who keep it, that the willing and obedient will eat the good of the land. There is always a reward for those who obey God. That was why God blessed Israel during his reign because he was willing to obey Him.
His son Solomon chose not to walk in God's Word in spite of all the wisdom he had. However, towards the end of his life, he gave a summary of how you and I should live.
"Let us hear the conclusion of the whole matter: Fear God, and keep his commandments: for this is the whole *duty* of man" (Ecclesiastes 12:13).

This means that he realized how good it was for him to have obeyed God and His Word. God warned the Israelites that they should not have many wives and they should not worship idols. "I will set a king over me like all the nations that around me,' you shall surely set a king over you... Neither shall he multiply wives for himself, lest his heart turn away; nor shall he greatly multiply silver and gold for himself" (Deuteronomy 17:14-17).

They were supposed to make God the center of their lives. King Solomon disobeyed God and broke all of those laws. God and His Word are one, therefore they can't be separated. You can't say you love God but you don't like or keep His Word.

The Word of God is spirit but it became flesh and lived among men. "In the beginning was the Word, and the Word was with God, and the Word was God. He was in the beginning with God.

All things were made through Him, and without Him nothing was made that was made. In Him was life, and the life was the light of men. And the light shines in the darkness, and the darkness did not comprehend it" (John 1:1-5).

The Word of God is Jesus. The Word of God is life because the Lord Jesus is life to the world. He told the multitude that His word is spirit and life. It is the Spirit who gives life; the flesh profits nothing. The words that I speak to you are spirit, and they are life (John 6:63).

The Scriptures says man shall not live by bread alone but by the Word of God. Which means the Word of God is life to the dying and perishing soul.

The Word of God is true, because the Lord Jesus is the Truth. When you know the truth you will be set free from all the lies of Satan. He is the Way to the Father. Jesus is the same yesterday, today and forever, which means He hasn't changed. God doesn't change either.

David knew that God's word remains the same. He knew that there is a resurrection of the dead. He encouraged himself when no one was there for him. He therefore comforted himself with the Word of God when his wedlock son died. "So David arose from the ground, washed and anointed himself, and changed his clothes; and he went into the house of the LORD and worshiped. Then he went to his own house; and when he requested, they set food before him, and he ate.

Then his servants said to him, "What is this that you have done? You fasted and wept for the child while *he was* alive, but when the child died, you arose and ate food."

And he said, "While the child was alive, I fasted and wept; for I said, 'Who can tell *whether* the LORD will be gracious to me, that the child may live?' But now he is dead; why should I fast? Can I bring him back again? I shall go to him, but he shall not return to me (2 Samuel 12: 20-23).

From the story above it can be concluded that David knew that there is eternal life. He was a student of the Word. Because King David loved God and the written word of God he had a revelation about the Lord Jesus than any of the kings of Israel. He wrote several songs about Him. It is spirit to spirit; the Spirit bears witness that we are the children of God, his spirit was really close to the Spirit of God.

He wrote:
"I am poured out like water,
And all My bones are out of joint;
My heart is like wax;
It has melted within Me.

118

My strength is dried up like a potsherd,

And My tongue clings to My jaws;
You have brought Me to the dust of death.
For dogs have surrounded Me;
The congregation of the wicked has enclosed Me.

They pierced My hands and My feet;
I can count all My bones.
They look *and* stare at Me.
They divide My garments among them,
And for My clothing they cast lots" (Psalm 22:14-18).

This was about the Messiah, Jesus. Even though a lot of the prophecies about the Messiah were written by Isaiah, Daniel and others after the death of King David, yet he knew that the Messiah would be coming.

He also wrote about the Messiah in Psalm 110. The Jews in the Lord Jesus' days on earth knew that the Messiah would come from the house of David because God had promised even through David's forefather Judah. Jacob pronounced a blessing on Judah that the scepter (authority or kingship) would not depart from his house.

King David began to rule in 1010 B.C. and the Prophet Isaiah started his ministry around 740 B.C. Isaiah wrote a lot about the Messiah as well (Isaiah 7, 9, 11, 42, 53, etc).

There was a story of a blind man who called on the Lord for healing He called Him Son of David. "Now as they came to Jericho, He went out of Jericho with His disciples and a great multitude, blind Bartimaeus, the son of Timaeus, sat by the road begging. And when he heard that it was Jesus of Nazareth, he began to cry out and say, 'Jesus, Son of David, have mercy on me!'" That meant most of them accepted the Word of God that He was the Son of David. (Luke 18: 35-42)

There was a dialogue between the Lord Jesus and the scribes (teachers of the Word). "Then Jesus answered and said, while He taught in the temple, "How is it that the scribes say that the Christ is the Son of David? For David himself said by the Holy Spirit:

'The LORD said to my Lord,
"Sit at My right hand,
Till I make Your enemies Your footstool."'

Therefore David himself calls Him 'Lord'; how is He then his Son?" And the common people heard Him" (Mark 12: 35-37).

King David wrote quite a lot of the entire book of Psalms; it is recorded that he wrote seventy three of the entire one hundred and fifty Psalms, though he is also accredited to some of the anonymous ones (by the Latin Vulgate and Septuagint). Almost all his songs were based on life-related stories. However, most importantly God or His Word was magnified. For instance, he wrote the following in one of his songs. "I will worship toward Your holy Temple and praise Thy Name for thy loving kindness and for thy truth: for thou hast magnified thy Word above all thy Name.

King David knew that the Word of God doesn't return void, but it would accomplish and achieve every purpose for which it was sent. That was why he wrote, "The Words of the LORD are pure words: *as* silver tried in a furnace of earth, purified seven times." This means God's words are flawless.

It is easier for even the heavens and the earth to pass away than for God's word not to be fulfilled. When God speaks He really means it. How do you see God's Word? Both written and spoken. Do you take it as serious as you should, or do you doubt it? David wrote about the voice of the LORD; it is full of Majesty, power, shakes the wilderness etc, (Psalm 29).

The Word of God is living and active and is sharper than any two edged sword. The Word counsels and helps us to stand firm in times of trails. David would have fainted but for the sake of the Word he stood firm. "I had fainted, unless I had believed to see the goodness of the LORD in the land of the living."

The Word of God is also called the Sword of the Spirit (Ephesians 6:17).

Kind David had a sword. He even took the sword of Goliath after killing him (1 Samuel 17:51, 21:9). He knew how important the sword was as an offensive and defensive weapon. Are we using our sword of the spirit as we are supposed to? If not we need to take it now so that we can defeat the devil, our enemy.

Because King David knew the Word of God and lived in it, he knew how dangerous it was to touch the Lord's anointed ones. He wrote Psalm 105:15 "Do not touch my anointed ones; do my prophets no harm."

Anointed means someone or something set apart for a divine purpose. Christ is the "Anointed One" Every child of God is anointed (though at different levels depending on what God wants us to do or how desperate we are for Him) because He lives in us. It was for that reason why he didn't touch King Saul.

David had the spiritual DNA of God. The Word of God was active in him, because he believed in God to the level that God made His dwelling with David.

Some people know the Word of God probably more than King David but they do not mix it with faith therefore making the Word of God powerless: that is religion and not true relationship.

David's prayer life persevered him until he received answers from God. because he realized that God and His Word are One. God has even exalted His Word above His Name.

Here are some few points on the Word of God you may want to memorized. Remember the "I"s. It is Immutable (Hebrew 6: 8, Infallible (Proverb 30:5-6). It Instructs, Inspires (2Timothy3:6-7)

It brings Illumination (Psalm 119:130), Integrity(Proverb 13:6, Psalm 84:11). It gives you and I a new Identity(1 Corinthians 6:20, John 1:12).

The Word of God washes us; it sanctifies it. Sanctify them by Your truth. Your word is truth (John 17:17). You are already clean because of the word which I have spoken to you(John 15:3),

When David sinned against God he wrote " purge me with hyssop and I shall be cleaned"(Psalm 51:7). We don't use hyssop anymore however, we are being sanctified by the Truth in the Word. Therefore when we sin we must repent and confess like David did and the Word of God that created all things would invade into our life and make us whole.

The Word of God is a weapon. A judge or an attorney must know the Law in order to defend others or himself so every believer must know the Book of the Law . It's your Weapon!

Personal Notes

The True worshippers of God must worship Him in spirit and in truth.- John 4:24.

Chapter 6

A True Worshipper
Food for your Soul and Spirit

Your spirit has an appetite for certain foods just as your body craves for certain foods for nourishment. Have you ever thought about that? If not I'm quite sure you will find some answers to this question.

God made man in three entities or beings according to Scripture: the spirit, soul and body.
"And the very God of peace sanctify you wholly; and I pray God your whole spirit and soul and body be preserved blameless unto the coming of our Lord Jesus Christ" (1 Thessalonians 5:23).

The body is obviously the physical being that we see, while the spirit and the soul are invisible and usually function together. It is a person's spirit that gives life, not the body. The moment the spirit leaves, the body no longer has life. Your soul departs the body with the spirit. Your soul consists of your emotions, will and intellect.

The spirit in everyone longs for its creator because there is a curiosity of how the universe came into existence. The question that needs to be asked: Is there a Supreme Being?

There is a sense of emptiness in every person who does not have a personal relationship with God through Jesus Christ. This is because God created man in His image with the purpose of man worshipping Him. God created man for Himself, He loves man so much that He would do everything to save man.

Man marred the relationship when he sinned against God in the Garden of Eden (Genesis 3). Man rebelled against God by eating the tree of the knowledge of good and evil. However, because God is mindful of man as King David wrote in one of his songs, He promised restoration. (Genesis 3:15).
"What is man that You are mindful of him,
And the son of man that You visit him?
For You have made him a little lower than the angels,
And You have crowned him with glory and honor" (Psalm 8:2).

God sent His Son the Lord Jesus to come and reconcile man to Him. He was a sacrificial Lamb that was killed for all the sins of man because there is no forgiveness of sin without the shedding of blood (Hebrews 8:22; Leviticus 17:11).

His death ultimately stops the wrath of God on a sinful man. The moment someone receives Christ as Lord and Savior the gap between God and man is closed. Then the Holy Spirit comes and dwells in your spirit and draws you closer to God. Your spirit can be satisfied that the cord once broken is now restored.

Spirit to spirit and flesh to flesh! (The spirit of man understands spiritual things the moment it is united with the Spirit of God). Worship is food for the spirit. The emptiness in man is filled when his spirit is reconnected to God in worship, because that was why he was created.

'Everyone who is called by My name,
Whom I have created for My glory;
I have formed him, yes, I have made him" (Isaiah 43:7).

Let us hear the conclusion of the whole matter: "Fear God, and keep his commandments: for this is the whole duty of man (Ecclesiastes 12:13).

The flesh weakens when the spirit of man cannot worship God. You become spiritually dry with the absence of the Holy Spirit. We try to fill our emptiness with drugs, getting drunk on alcohol, sexual immorality, money, etc. which of course can't fill the emptiness. It's like putting a round peg into a square hole. It doesn't work because Jesus is the answer to the emptiness!

As we have learned from Scripture; King David was the son of Jesse a descendant of Judah and the Prophet Isaiah also prophesied about the Messiah that would come from the root of Jesse from the tribe of Judah whose Kingdom would reign forever and ever (Isaiah 11:1).

Please read the genealogy of Jesus in the Bible (Matthew 1:1-17, Luke 3:23-38).

David wrote one of his songs while he was in the wilderness of Judah, "O God you are my God, earnestly: I seek for you; my soul thirsts for you my flesh faints for you, as in a dry and weary land where there is no water" (Psalm 63:1).

From the above scripture one can see that Kind David was at a place where he couldn't worship God. His soul was thirsting for God which was proof that his spirit was very dry.

As discussed earlier, we learned that our soul is our will, emotion and intellect. Your soul makes decisions and experiences thoughts and feelings that affect your spirit and eventually affects the body.

For instance when you decide to get drunk because of loneliness your spirit will still be empty as long as your spirit is not saved (redeemed by the Blood of Jesus). You may be happy for a short period but, after a while you would come back to your sadness. Emotionally, your feelings can be fragmented and physical challenges leading to depression and sickness can manifest in the long run.

The only solution would be the Spirit of God filling the emptiness with joy so that there would be no room for sadness.

If you experience the trauma of King David as written in the book of Psalms, you would understand the emotions, thoughts, and decisions his inner man went through. I'm sure it was hard for David' when his son Absalom conquered him as King over Israel, exiling David with the help of one of David's personal advisor's (2 Samuel 15).

While hiding from his son in the wilderness, David missed worshiping God in the palace and also congregational worship. Which leads us to the next question: What then is worship?

Is it something that goes on during a religious service? Does it happen during the day? Is it about singing and celebration? Is it an event? Does it affect your lifestyle, etc.?

Worship comes from two English words. The combined words are "worth" and "ship" which then make up "worthship" which means to ascribe quality of having worthy or the quality of being worthy.

As we look at David's life we can learn about this passion of worship that he experienced! King David was a worshiper in God's sight. He had communion with God often and God is spirit. His worship was spirit to spirit; the spirit of man connecting to the Spirit of God.

God is looking for the same from us. God wants us to worship Him with all that we have and all that we are. Scripture tells us that Cain killed Abel because both of them offered a sacrifice to God but God accepted Abel's and rejected Cain's. Abel offered and worshiped God wholeheartedly. Because He is the Ultimate Creator we have to be ready to choose His will over our own.

Loving God with all our heart, soul, mind and strength, makes it very easy for us to worship Him in spirit and in truth. King David knew this from his youth and he lived it.

Worshipping is a position or posture where we align our hearts and spirits in submission to God. The center of every worshipper is love. We will definitely know how to worship God if we love Him. It is to love Him with all our hearts, soul and mind and strength.

The Lord Jesus said you will obey Him if you love Him (John 14:15). Therefore obedience can be a key to worship. Obedience is a choice that each person has the option to make. God will never force any one to obey Him but at the end of the day we are responsible for the choices we make. Therefore, "to obey is better that sacrifice" (1 Samuel 15:22).

Worshipping God in spirit and in truth takes us to the story of a woman at the well of Jacob.

This woman had five men in her life and none of them were her husband. She went to the well to fetch water and behold the Lord was sitting at the well by Himself. A dialogue took place between them and the Lord said "But the hour is coming, and now is, when the true worshipers will worship the Father in spirit and truth; for the Father is seeking such to worship Him. God *is* Spirit, and those who worship Him must worship in spirit and truth" (John 4:23-24).

The Jews used to worship God on mount Zion, in the Tabernacle, Temple, or the Synagogue (the Synagogue is a smaller place of assembly compared to the Temple). But the Lord said we don't have to worship God on the mountain because His Spirit was going to dwell in man and also dwell with man.

It is just like saying we don't have to go to the Church, cell groups, or house fellowships before we can worship God. You can worship wherever you are. Isn't that amazing?!

The Tabernacle, mountain, Temple, or Synagogue was the meeting place with God, His house or His presence. Now, the New Testament describes your body as being the temple of the Holy Spirit. If your body is the temple then God expects you to use it for the right purpose. It takes a purpose-driven life to surrender your whole life to God so you can avoid unnecessary misery.

Therefore, true worship deals with more than your geographical location (although important at times). It is even more important to acknowledge the Creator, as you surrender your spirit, soul and body to Him to bring God glory and honor and also benefit the common good of all men. This means yielding your will to God's will.

God does not need man to worship Him for Him to be the Supreme Being and the Creator of All Things. However, He loves it when people will freely worship Him from the depths of their heart as King David did. He created man to worship him because He takes delight in man while Satan fights hard to destroy man. Satan or Lucifer wanted to be worshipped as God. He therefore rebelled against God causing many of the angels to fall (Isaiah 14:12; 2 Peter 2:4; Revelation 12:7-9).

Michael the Archangel fought against him and cast him out of Heaven and on to the earth. Satan's throne is therefore on the earth and the second heaven. We have three heavens. The first one is where we see the earth atmosphere like birds, etc, the second heaven is the outer space starry heavens and the third is where God's throne is.

Since God created the world, He alone is to be worshipped and not creation as we read in the first two of the Ten Commandments:

"I *am* the LORD your God, who brought you out of the land of Egypt, out of the house of bondage.
"You shall have no other gods before Me.
"You shall not make for yourself a carved image—any likeness *of anything* that *is* in heaven above, or that *is* in the earth beneath, or that *is* in the water under the earth; you shall not bow down to them nor serve them. For I, the LORD your God, *am* a jealous God, visiting the iniquity of the fathers upon the children to the third and fourth *generations* of those who hate Me, but showing mercy to thousands, to those who love Me and keep My commandments."

Exodus 20:1-6

If we obey God it produces good consequences; because man reaps whatever he sows. It is a law in the Kingdom of God. However, if you sow to the flesh, you will reap evil and if you sow in the spirit you reap in the spirit (Galatians 6:7).

The Bible tells us that Paul wrote to the Church in Rome that men chose to honor created things instead of God because of pride,

131

therefore God gave them over to a deprived mind (Romans 1:22-26). This means if you worship the creation instead of the Creator, you won't have the mind to receive the specific benefits and blessing of God created for you on earth and in eternity.

David honored and memorized the Ten Commandments and most of the civil and customary laws by heart because it represented his worship to God.

The first of the Ten Commandments; "Thou shalt have no other gods before Me" states clearly that God is a jealous God. He doesn't want you to worship or serve any other god besides Him.

King David knew God was his source of power and confessed it openly. In his last days he wrote in a song of praise how he was entangled with death, yet he cried out to God and He delivered him (2 Samuel 22). In fact, there were several times David had to cry out to God during his life (other instances can be found in Psalms 18:6, 34:17).

He was an expert harp player and he used this anointing to provide relief for King Saul whenever Saul was being tormented by an evil spirit (1 Samuel 16:23). The evil spirits tormenting Saul could not stand this anointed worship on David and his harp.

When we worship with instruments, the sounds of those instruments become repellant to the demons. They get confused and tormented especially when the person playing is anointed or filled with the power of God. Have you ever imagined the frequencies of the sounds of the instruments they play at Church?

Some people don't like instruments. They always want maybe just a quiet note on the piano. There are all kinds of instruments in Heaven praising God therefore we have to get use to it like the Psalmist wrote (Psalm 150).

The favor of God upon David's life brought enmity and war between his house and King Saul's, but because David was a true worshipper his house grew stronger and stronger while Saul's house grew weaker and weaker (2 Samuel 3:1).

David's worship manifested through his writings, instruments and singing. He certainly knew how to sing. Many Church worship teams have members who can sing with angelic voices, but that doesn't make them worshippers. Singing without the Holy Spirit is not worship!

Worshippers worship even when no one is around, but "performers" are performance oriented and need human appraisal. Worshipers direct their attention to God; "performers" direct their attention to themselves.

The Levites were one of the tribes of Israel. Their duty was to serve God and the people because they were the Priests. They were faithful with their duties and served whether people were there or not; they realized it was their duty.

True worshipers worship God wherever they are and under all circumstances, night or day. They do not wait for someone to tell them to lift their hands or open their mouths to worship God. It's in their DNA. If the devil can keep you silent and your hands folded he can disarm you. Worship is our weapon of protection.

Oh may we be like the Levites, always on our posts as true worshippers of God.

King David knew the importance of the presence of God. He definitely knew that money couldn't buy it and he couldn't live without it. He was willing to pay whatever he needed to keep the anointing on him. That was why he was a good worshiper. Every believer's desire should be to want more of God's presence. Worship deals with the heart.

Sometimes you can worship something or someone without necessarily realizing what you are doing. Whatever you give the greatest respect becomes your "god."

David gave the highest esteem to God in his heart and life. Scripture says "Out of the overflow of the heart the mouth speaks." (Matthew 12:34). David's heart was full of God and worship was the end product of his passion.

Your body cannot be empty; it must be filled with a spirit. Your spirit will either be alive to God or the world and the devil. A worldly spirit will drive you to materialism. If the Spirit of God leaves a body, another spirit takes over.
If God's Spirit is absent, the only other choice is an evil spirit or the spirit of the world. For instance, an empty bottle is filled with air even though you think it's empty. The moment you fill it with water the air is displaced.

The spirit of man is empty like the bottle because of the fall of Adam and Eve in the Garden of Eden (Genesis 3). When you accept Jesus as Lord and Savior, God's Spirit comes and dwells in you; you are righteous! If you go back to the old sin the evil spirits that were in you would come back with seven wicked ones and your condition or lifestyle will be worse than it was before (Matthew 12:43).

The spirit of a Christian or a righteous person cannot be possessed by the devil. The spirit becomes renewed or reborn the moment you accept the Lord into your heart. Your soul and body can be possessed or oppressed (tormented) by the devil. The more you grow spiritually by conforming to Christ in the renewing of the mind, the less chance the devil has control over your soul and body.

In the Old Testament, righteousness came by the law because Jesus had not yet incarnated as God in the form of man. David was righteous in God's sight. He had communion with God.

Everyone can praise God, but not everyone can worship God. Praise is exalting God and showing Him our appreciation for all that He has done. It is applauding Him for His mighty works.

A form of worship is bending on your knees before God, lifting your hands to God, and telling Him the reason you live is to worship Him. God always shows up and gives us the grace we need. He is honored when you worship and praise Him.

King David understood these concepts. It was therefore easy for him to worship God wherever he was and in every challenge he faced. God always manifests Himself in our situation when we sincerely worship Him from our hearts.

It is no coincidence that David was a worshiper who knew how to praise God. We know that David was a musician and a dancer. He was from the tribe of Judah (Praise) and Judah was one of Jacob's sons.

King David therefore fulfilled the prophetic word from his forefather Jacob that the scepter of kingship would not depart from Judah's linage. They would be worshippers (Genesis 49:8-10).

King David was a worshiper to be emulated. He loved God with all his heart, soul, mind and strength. It was very easy for him to worship God as the Scripture says "in spirit and in truth."

King David practiced this from his childhood. How serious are you with your worship to God? Do you give him the best of your time, resources, heart and life? If you are sincere in worshiping God in truth, you will serve him with all that you have!

And like David we all have prophetic destinies, even though we have been called to different spheres of influence in life... for instance the media, government etc to proclaim Christ. Not until we worship God sincerely from the heart those prophecies will not come to pass.

Personal prophecies are conditional (IF). Example is "If My people, who are called by My name, shall humble themselves, pray, seek, crave, *and* require of necessity My face and turn from their wicked ways, then will I hear from heaven, forgive their sin, and heal their land (2 Chronicles 7:14).

Because King David was a true worshiper, God would show up whenever he worshiped. Because he tried to create the right atmosphere and dwelling place prepared for God to inhabit, God was warmly welcomed! We will experience the presence of God when we create the right atmosphere for Him. His Spirit is very gentle and will not force His way into our life till we invite Him. "Behold, I stand at the door and knock. If anyone hears My voice and opens the door, I will come in to him and eat with him, and he with Me" (Revelation 3:20).

Worship is acknowledging the Deity and Supremacy of God. A prideful heart is self-seeking, self-righteous and non-submissive. But even as a King, David was humble in his heart. He knew it was by the grace of God that he was King and that he didn't deserve it.

Sometimes when God promotes us or blesses us with possessions, we give more attention to positions and possessions instead of God. The more you make God your priority the easier it is for Him to promote you and provide for you.

If you give more attention to things than you do God, you will fall into the same temptations the Israelites experienced. The heathen (pagan) nations amongst Israel worshipped many different kinds of idols and gods. But God commanded the Israelites in the Ten Commandments not to worship any other god besides Him.

"You shall not make for yourself an image in the form of anything in heaven above, or on earth beneath or in the water below. You shall not bow down to or worship them for I the Lord your God am a jealous God punishing the children for the sins of the parents to the third and fourth generation of those who hate me, but showing love to a thousand generation of those who love me, and keep my commandment" (Deuteronomy 5:8-10).

In spite of all those warnings from God, sadly enough the Israelites did not fully destroy them but even intermarried with the pagans. That caused them to pollute their true worship because they even practiced human sacrifice whereby they sacrificed their children to idols. God became angry with the Israelites. The Israelites were a nation under one God (Theocracy). But because they mingled with the gods of other nations, they became a nation with many gods.

After many years of pagan worship, David's heart was to bring them back to worshiping the one and true God. They did not maintain their worship to God after the death of Moses and Joshua which was during the Israelites forty-year wilderness journey from Egypt. It all started when the Israelites were pressured to make a golden calf as a god.

It did not end there. They became more corrupted during the rule of the judges, prior to the era of the rule of Kings. Saul was the first King and continued the idol worship by consulting sorceress which was an abomination to God (1 Samuel 28). David succeeded King Saul, and Solomon succeeded David.

Because David was a true worshipper and had the dream of bringing the nation of Israel under One God, he decided to build the Temple for God where they would worship Him day and night. Though David didn't build the Temple, he laid the pattern of worship for his son Solomon and the congregation to build as discussed earlier. He would have loved to build it but God did not permit it because his hands were filled with blood from being a warrior. Because he was a zealous warrior who had zero tolerance for idols in the Kingdom.

King David was anointed and was chosen by God to turn the hearts of the people from idols to the One and True God through genuine worship. True Worship in Israel did not last after his son King Solomon succeeded him because he married many foreign wives who brought their pagan worship to Israel and turned his heart from God to idol worshipping. In spite of all his wisdom, he allowed lust to drive him into deep sin.

The Word of God is true, when the righteous are in authority the people rejoice, but when the wicked rules the people groan (Proverbs 29:2). Israel was blessed because of King David. His son King Solomon brought a reproach to the nation of Israel. God wants His children to intercede for people in authority in our nations so that they would worship Him and rule with righteousness and justice, because these are the foundations of His throne!

David's heart of true worship gave birth to something significant we can see in our generation. He loved God so much that he wanted to build a "24/7 House of Prayer" for the Israelites to worship God day and night. He worshipped God with all his heart, time, resources, talent, finances etc.

We see a lot of Prayer Houses being birthed out of King David's vision. The International House of Prayer in Kansas City (IHOP), Pasadena International House of Prayer,(PIHOP) Pasadena, Radiance International House of Prayer in West Hollywood, Los Angeles, Sunrise House of Prayer in Alhambra, CA and many others across the globe. They are all prototypes of what King David's envisioned. God has promised to restore the true pattern of worship before the end of the world (Amos 9:11, Acts 15:16). God wants the candles or "fire" to be burning day and night in His house. God instructed Moses to keep the candle burring. It stands for divine understanding of the Word of God and worship.

King David had a contrite heart. A contrite heart comes before God in humility and worship even when God disciplines. He wrote in Psalm 15, "Lord who shall abide in thy tabernacle? Who shall dwell in thy holy hill? He that walketh uprightly worketh righteousness, and speaketh the truth in his heart. He that backbiteth not with his tongue, nor doeth evil to his neighbor" (Psalm 15:1-3, KJV).

This is an inspirational Scripture you should meditate on. You are righteous if you believe in Jesus as your Savior. The children of God are the righteousness of God through Jesus. Hence, the moment you become a follower of Christ, you have right standing with God. In the Old Testament righteousness was determined by reverence to God and keeping the laws

Therefore, the righteous should have no problems worshiping God in spirit and truth.

During the Old Testament times, there were instances unrighteous men tried to worship God in their own ways and God brought judgment on them. God warned them, but they chose what they thought was right and lost their life.

Among those were the sons of Eli who was a High Priest in Shiloh before the Prophet Samuel was born. His sons were Hopni and Phinehas. They were spoiled and ate portions of meat which were to be sacrificed to God. They also slept with the women at the entrance of the tent. Though they knew the right way of worshipping God they didn't worship or reverence Him. God struck both of them dead! (1 Samuel 2:12-36). Knowing the right thing to do but failing to do is sin (James 4:17).

How would God deal with us today if we were committing similar sins and the Holy Spirit's conviction did not cause us to listen and repent, but rather we hardened our hearts?

Hopefully, we would quickly repent because God is always in the business of restoration. He desires us all to be saved and He loves to see us run to him with a sincere heart.

With the story of Eli we learn that we need to teach our children the Word of God; how to worship and live a holy lifestyle. Sometimes we are so busy serving the Lord we leave our household unattended. That is not good.

King David wrote "I will bless the Lord at all times. His praise shall continually be on my lips (Psalm 34:1-2). He worshipped the Lord in the field or at his "job," in his tent or at his "house." He worshipped God during rain or shine; as long as it was a new day. We can also worship God anywhere and at anytime.

As the Lord told the Samaritan woman at the well, they would no longer go to the mountains to worship. He also added that the Samaritans worship what they don't know. That's true some people worship what they don't know. The Samaritans didn't know their God according to the dialogue the Lord had with the woman at the well, "You Samaritans worship what you do not know; we worship what we do know, for salvation is from the Jews" (John 4:22).

The Samaritans were considered half-breeds because they intermarried cross culture. They were Jews originally, but after the Israelites went into captivity, the nations like the Assyrians and the

141

Babylonians took the healthiest slaves and left the weak ones there. Then they brought some of the pagan nations to occupy the land. As time passed and the Jews intermarried, they ceased from practicing the Jewish culture. They mixed their culture and beliefs to the point that pure Jews no longer respected them.

Also in the book of Acts we read how Paul was on his mission trip to Athens and saw the people in Athens worshipping an idol "To the Unknown god." He took that opportunity to share the Gospel with them. Some rejected him and others were willing to hear him again (Acts 17:23-33).

The people who know their God and worship Him in spirit and in truth shall do exploits because it's a privilege to know Him.

Worshipping God is not only at a Synagogue or in Jerusalem. Likewise, it is not only on Sundays, midweek services, or Saturdays for the Adventists however, it is every day for those in Christ. Worshipping could be in the morning, noon, evenings, nights or dawn.

Jonah prayed and worshipped God in the belly of the whale, and God heard him (Jonah 2:1-9). King David knew God and he believed that God knew him so he couldn't hide from God (Psalm 56, 139: 7-12).

So we are not limited to worship anywhere. I worship in my mind while I am working or doing the house chores and sometimes sing very quietly.

Our worship can be in a song, hymns or we can worship God with a new song. We see the "New Song" in some of the songs in the book of Psalms. For instance, Psalms 33:3 talks about singing a new song unto the Lord.

A new song is a song that one composes as the Holy Spirit leads or inspires you; without the help of an experienced composer or a song writer. When the saints sing a new song it is like the sweet aroma in God's nostrils, because it comes from clean vessels and it is sung with love and faith.

We sing a new song out of an overflow of joy. Every worshipper eventually knows how to sing a new song. Sing to the LORD a new song; sing to the LORD, all the earth (Psalm 96:1).

David was an expert in singing a new song to the Lord. Your spirit joins with that of God's Spirit and the words are anointed. How often do you sing a new song to the Lord? God opens the heavens and gives us visions about his plans and purposes during times of worship.

Like King David, be vigilant and worship throughout your day. Some of David's best worship Psalms were written while watching over his sheep.

Some find it easier to worship corporately, while others individually, but both have their place. During corporate worship there is a more powerful anointing. As we pray and worship in unison; power is unleashed, yokes destroyed, burdens removed and miracles take place because of the corporate anointing. This corporate worship should be our lifestyle because God is a relational Person. You don't have to stay home and not be connected to a local church unless for health issues or your geographic location makes it impossible for you to join a local Church, etc.

King David was connected to the congregation of God's people. We have to be accountable to one another therefore being in a community makes it quite easy for the saints.

While there is an easy element in worshiping together, God also loves intimate worship with us individually. Salvation is personal so individual worship is equally important to God. He is giving every soul an opportunity to come to the saving knowledge of Christ and worship Him in an appropriate way.

Since it is a bit hard to worship individually, it is wise to find a way of making it part of you. A very simple and enriching way to worship God is to join along on CDs, the internet or with sheet music. As you play songs, worship, thank God and express your gratitude. See in your mind the image of a child standing next to mom and dad. The child stands reaching out to the parent in a display of love.

Let the Holy Spirit lead and guide you, and He can bring a new song to your soul. Do not be in such a rush when in His presence. And at the same time we shouldn't neglect our duties and responsibilities with the excuse of worshipping. God wants us to have a spirit of excellent and wisdom.

We must schedule our time so that we will have at least 15 minutes in the mornings for Him. I normally plan at least half hour. I know some people have very busy daily routine, the kids; their schooling, their house chores, family issues, jobs and spouses, etc. We can get at least 10-15 minutes daily worship before we leave home. When we have few minutes of worship before we start our day, that would be the foundation for us to build on for the day as we work, drive etc.

True worshippers like King David are contagious because they carry the very essence of God's glory everywhere. They are like a magnet ready to snatch up a pile of nails.

Only true worshippers can have real intimacy with God, because we must be naked and transparent before Him. Our transparency with Him will be evident to all men because men would recognize us through our fruit. Because a tree is recognized by its fruits.

I think true worshippers are people that we really have to fear besides God, because they have the heart of God and hear His heart beat. I could say they are people who really love God. You cannot tell me that you love God but would not like to obey Him; that is a lie says the scripture.

True worshippers honor, acknowledge God, they fear or reverence Him. They definitely love Him and keep His Word. They are transparent even when they sin against God they repent and turn to God wholeheartedly like King David. Because God's word is true, He honors those who honor Him and has a special care for such people.

The Psalmist wrote "He who dwells in the shelter of the Most High shall abide under the shadow of the Almighty." Psalm 91:1. God desires to have an intimate relationship with man, so that He would reveal Himself in a progressive way to man.

God is unfathomable, but the more we draw closer each day the more we get to know Him more.

"Because he hath set his love upon me, therefore will I deliver him:(deliverance). I will set him on high, because he hath known my name. (promotion) He shall call upon me, and I will answer him:(favor, providence) I *will be* with him in trouble; (protection). I will deliver him, and honor him. (favor, honor). With long life will I satisfy him, and shew him my salvation (Psalm 91:14-16).

These are some the promises of God for the true worshippers: Deliverance, promotion, protection, providence and longevity. Even though not all true worshippers live long for some reasons, yet each of them fulfills their purpose here on earth. Don't you want to inherit these promises? The choice is in our hands.

In conclusion, God and His Word are true therefore He wants us to worship Him in spirit and in truth. The spirit of man is seeking for its creator! Its desire would be fulfilled by reconnecting to the Spirit of the Creator.

King David worshipped God wholeheartedly, the fathers of faith we read in the Bible or the early church who loved God did likewise. There is therefore no exception for you and I if we desire to know God a closer way. He who wants to be the greatest of all must be the servant of all. The way up is the way down as the saying goes We worship God because we love Him. Worshipping God is not a punishment but a privilege!

Personal Notes.

David was a relentless warrior!

Lesson 7

A Warrior and an Intercessor

Living as a gap builder.

An intercessor is someone who stands in the "gap" for others and sees that God's grace, mercy and justice are executed for the oppressed. In the Old Testament days they had Prophets and Priests who interceded for the nation and individuals.

Our world is made up of different personalities. If you took an IQ test of a dozen people like my twelve brothers and sisters, you would have equally different types of personalities, even though they have the same parents. Some of them are introvert and others are extrovert.

However, all types of personalities are unique and each is important. For instance in sports, teams have defenses and offenses to make up a good team.

David was someone who was always at the warfront. He was known as a great warrior and an intercessor. The only time the Bible records King David being behind enemy lines was when he committed adultery with Bathsheba.

"It happened in the spring of the year, during the time kings go out *to battle* that David sent Joab and his servants with him, and all Israel; and they destroyed the people of Ammon and besieged Rabbah. But David remained at Jerusalem. Then it happened one evening that David arose from his bed and walked on the roof of the king's house. And from the roof he saw a woman bathing, and the woman *was* very beautiful to behold.

So David sent and inquired about the woman. And *someone* said, "*Is* this not Bathsheba, the daughter of Eliam, the wife of Uriah the Hittite?" Then David sent messengers, and took her; and she came to him, and he lay with her, for she was cleansed from her impurity; and she returned to her house (2 Samuel 11:1-4, NKJV).

If David were at the warfront doing what he does best and involved in God's will, he probably wouldn't have been in a position of temptation.

He fought many wars and interceded for the Israelites when they were being harassed or oppressed by their enemies (for example the Philistines (1 Samuel 17) and the Amalekites (1 Samuel 30).

He was a warrior trained by God. A warrior is a man engaged or experienced in warfare; broadly: a person engaged in some

148

struggle or conflict. A warrior does not usually need to be dispatched for war like the soldier. The difference between a warrior and a soldier is that the warrior has battlefield experience and a thirst for warfare while a soldier is someone who is trained but not necessarily tested in battle.

David was always optimistic as a warrior, because he knew his relationship with the Lord was really strong and that made him confident that no one could defeat him without God's consent.

The Bible tells us that we war not against the flesh and the blood like King David did in the Old Testament. We war against Satan and his evil spirits. Since we approach war differently in the New Testament, instead of the physical warfare of King David, we have prayer warriors. Our warfare is not physical but spiritual.

"Finally, my brethren, be strong in the Lord and in the power of His might. Put on the whole armor of God that you may be able to stand against the wiles of the devil. For we do not wrestle against flesh and blood, but against principalities, against powers, against the rulers of the darkness of this age, against spiritual *hosts* of wickedness in the heavenly places (Ephesians 6:10-12).

The Lord Jesus' death and resurrection has stripped Satan of his authority and God has delegated the authority and power to the followers of Christ to fight the good fight of faith in Jesus' Name (Satan has power but he has no authority.

The authority comes from God or people in high position though they all eventually come from God. It is the right someone has to execute something. Therefore we have to submit to people in authority because God placed them.

149

'Let everyone be subject to the governing authorities, for there is no authority except that which God has established. The authorities that exist have been established by God. Consequently, whoever rebels against the authority is rebelling against what God has instituted, and those who do so will bring judgment on themselves" (Romans 13:1-2).

A simple explanation of the difference between power and authority:

For instance, King David was authorized by King Saul to fight Goliath but he fought with the power of God in him.

King David was always willing to do the best for his nation as a King. Even though he always consulted the Prophets he always stood in the gap for the people.

An intercessor simply brings petitions of prayers to God on behalf of people. Intercessors never quit or get tired of bringing the petition before God because that is their nature. They could pray for decades about a situation or for an individual and would never quit till God intervenes.

Not everyone can be an intercessor but everyone can be a prayer warrior. It is easier for a prayer warrior than an intercessor to quit. An intercessor and a prayer warrior can be compared to long and short distant runners. The long distance runner has a mindset to endure to the finish line while the prayer warrior's mindset is "let's get it done now."

A prayer warrior could pray and shake the whole atmosphere but may not be able to maintain it for a long duration of time, while the intercessor is the very opposite. A prayer warrior can be compared to a short distance runner while an intercessor can be compared to a long distance runner.

As a warrior, David had the perseverance of an intercessor and continually stood in the gap to intercede for his nation.

He fought against his enemies till he completely destroyed them (2Samuel 22:38-43). For instance, before he fought and killed Goliath the story showed his brevity as he dialogued with King Saul "Moreover David said, "The LORD, who delivered me from the paw of the lion and from the paw of the bear, He will deliver me from the hand of this Philistine" (1 Samuel 17:37).

In that story David's father Jesse sent him to the battlefield to see how his older brothers were doing and provide food. He saw the horrifying situation his nation Israel was facing. He thought to himself he was born to kill the giant, so he stepped out beyond all obstacles to kill him. He fulfilled his dreams through the killing of Goliath.

As stated earlier, an intercessor is one who pleads on behalf of another person. The phrases, "bringing a request on" and "behalf of another" presents an interesting question. Why can't they pray for themselves?

In fact, we are encouraged to come boldly before the Throne of God with our request. "Let us therefore come boldly unto the throne of grace that we may obtain mercy, and find grace to help in time of need" (Hebrews 4:16).

Even though God has given the gift of intercessor to some, we all are called to cover one another in prayer.

According to the Scriptures God wants every believer to intercede for all men; for kings, queens, people of influence and authority so that they will all come to know the saving knowledge of God and know that God's Son Jesus is the Only Mediator between God and man.

Our prayers can help stand in the gap for those who have important decisions to make that affect the common good of all.

David interceded on behalf of God's people on many occasions. Once there was famine for three years and he prayed to God about why there was famine in the land. God revealed to him that it involved King Saul's killing of some Gibeonites (2 Samuel 21).

The Gibeonites were a tribe that made a pact or a covenant with the Israelites that they would serve them forever. They deceived the Israelites because they were afraid of them and their miracle working God who had parted the Red Sea. (Please read the story from Joshua 9).

King David pleaded to God that justice would be executed so that rain would fall on the land for his people. He did not want his people oppressed or God's Name blasphemed. Just as David was; I believe God has called each believer to be a warrior and intercessor.

Jesus is interceding for all believers in Heaven and He is coming back as a warrior (Isaiah 42:13). The Holy Spirit is also a warrior and He intercedes through us with groans (wailing and moaning in intercessory prayer).

The Holy Spirit intercedes through us with groans. Likewise the Spirit also helps in our weaknesses. "For we do not know what we should pray for as we ought, but the Spirit Himself makes intercession for us with groaning which cannot be uttered. Now He who searches the hearts knows what the mind of the Spirit *is,* because He makes intercession for the saints according to *the will of* God" (Romans 8:26-27).

The Holy Spirit does spiritual warfare through believers. Spiritual warfare is of course an invisible war in the spirit realm. He engages in a war with the angels of God on our behalf (2 Timothy 1: 14, Psalm 91:11, Luke 4:10). The reason Jesus came to earth was to destroy the works of the devil (1 John 3:8).

God has a unique relationship to the Jews and has been fighting on their behalf since He made a covenant with Abraham (Genesis 15:18). Jesus also has a unique relationship with the church and its often described as the "Bride of Christ." He will also be fighting for the Church until He returns. That is why He said:

"And I say unto thee. That thou art Peter, and upon this rock I will build my church and the gates of hell shall not prevail against it" (Matthew 16:18).

Because King David was both a prayer warrior and an intercessor he had a great compassion for souls. He was violently determined and persistent in whatever he did for the nation of Israel and God.

Every child of God has to be violently persistent for the Kingdom of God because you can never regain your possessions if you don't know how to fight the enemy. Though Satan is a defeated foe, he still fights back with deceptions and he is a thief, liar and a murderer (John 10:10).

"And from the days of John the Baptist until now the Kingdom of Heaven suffers violence, and the violent take it by force" (Matthew 11:12).

The Kingdom of God has suffered violence. This means we have to be consistent and persistent in fighting the good fight of faith.

The Holy Spirit is our Guide and Teacher. David won all his battles because he understood the battle is the Lord's and the real strength came not by might, power but by God's Spirit.

The Bible gives a brief record of King David's victories (2 Samuel 8). David recognized that God was the source of his victory. We also need to recognize that we are in a spiritual battle with armor and strategies to win the war. There is a spiritual warfare going on around us day and night. This war is between good and evil.

A prayer warrior and an intercessor must always be sensitive to the directions of the Holy Spirit. They both require the spirit of discernment. The discernment of spirits is one of the nine gifts of the Holy Spirit described in the book of Corinthians which helps us to differentiate between good and evil spirits (1Corithians 12:10).

God wants us to desire the gifts and use them to build up others and promote His Kingdom. Therefore we don't desire the gifts for the sake of boasting or wrongfully using them.

Since every believer has the Holy Spirit they should have the spirit of discernment to some extent. The Holy Spirit reveals things to come according to the Scripture (John 16:13).

We need to consult the Holy Spirit daily because we cannot live without His direction. Every warrior invading the enemy's territory needs an organized strategy from his supreme commander in order to win the war. With the Christians, the Commander is the Holy Spirit.

David as a young boy was led by the Spirit of God. He had a superior foe named Goliath. But David stood before the taunting Philistine captain and said "come here and I'll give your flesh to the birds of the air and the beast of the field" (1Samuel 17:44). Goliath underestimated David's strength by judging him according to his appearance and not his strength, which was the LORD. Therefore we shouldn't judge our enemy only by appearance.

King David never underestimated or judged his enemies potential but he based his strategies on the power of God. He knew his identity in God and he knew he was chosen as King of Israel. Talking of under-estimating the cost or the strength of the enemy, one can compare the cost the United States of America had paid in the past years on wars. Sometimes it's not worth to go to war if you count the cost!

Since our warfare are not carnal but mighty through God. And also by the new identity we have in God through Christ I think we should be more excited about our new identities. "We are a royal priesthood, a holy nation, a peculiar people chosen by God from darkness and into light to show His praises"(1 Peter 2:9).

We should be motivated by David's example to shake off every weight of heaviness and challenge and remind ourselves that we have an uncompromising mandate to accomplish; God's mission in our life. We should therefore see ourselves as gap-standers.

The Spirit of God spoke through the Prophet Isaiah "I have posted watchmen on your walls O Jerusalem; they will never be silent day or night. You who call on the LORD, give yourself no rest, and give Him no rest till He establishes Jerusalem and makes her the praise of the earth" (Isaiah 62:6-7).

In ancient days, every city had a wall. The city couldn't be defeated unless the walls were broken. The watchmen would guard the city from the city towers. They would sound trumpets when the enemy was coming to attack their city. They had gatemen who were responsible for securing and knowing who was coming in and out. During an attack all the men of war would run to the gates to fight the enemy.

When we act as an intercessor we are like watchmen and gatekeepers. We have the spiritual ability to see our enemy from a distance and we have the authority to allow the devil in or kick him out.

Throughout the Scriptures we see that God used many intercessors. We see Abraham interceding for Lot when God was going to destroy Sodom and Gomorrah (Genesis 18:20-33).

Moses' wife Zipporah interceded for him when God was going to strike Moses' son dead. Moses knew he should have circumcised his son on the eighth day after birth. For some reason he did not circumcise his son even though he knew the covenant of circumcision God made with Abraham for his entire descendants.

Moses had been in exile in Midian for killing an Egyptian, but being in a foreign land was not a reason for him to forget his covenant with God (Exodus 4:24-26).

We may also go through circumstances where we seem alone and without support. However, this should not deter us from being faithful to the Lord.

Even though Moses seemed unfaithful at times, God still chose him to intercede for the Israelites, when God became angry with their unfaithfulness and idol worship. God wanted to destroy them for their sin of unbelief and idolatry and made Moses a great nation. Possibly God might have raised children through Moses, but Moses interceded on their behalf and God spared their life (Exodus 32:10-14).

The Bible records several people who stood in the gap for the nation of Israel like King David. People like Joshua, Gideon, Esther, Nehemiah, Daniel and many more were intercessors.

The Lord Jesus is interceding for us right now according to the Scriptures (Hebrews 7:25). He also interceded for His disciples as well as all believers before He died (John 17:6-26).

The Lord interceded for Peter and he repented and was restored after the Lord's resurrection (Mark16:1-7). Abigail was one of King David's wives. Her ex-husband was Nabal, which means "a fool" acted like a fool." King David and his warriors were hungry and asked Nabal to feed his men but he refused to welcome them.

David could have killed Nabal and his entire household, but Abigail being a wise woman interceded for him and her household. God struck Nabal dead and after that King David married Abigail (1 Samuel 25). King David therefore knew the importance of intercession.

Love is the center of intercession. That's why the Lord Jesus said we should love our enemies and intercede for them. Every good intercessor is a loving and compassionate person. Every good intercessor must live a selfless life with a humble spirit like King David.

Love doesn't rejoice in evil. For example, if someone hates you and dies, would you rejoice or mourn? King David did not rejoice over the death of King Saul, but instead mourned for him. Yet, Saul's jealousy and insecurity took many attempts to kill David.

David had the same attitude as Jesus described by Paul the Apostle in the book of Philippians (Philippians 2:5-9). Every good intercessor must have a forgiving heart and a humble spirit because God is not pleased with pride.

How can you intercede for someone who hates you and wants to kill or destroy your life? Our Lord did it on the cross and Stephen did the same when he said, "Lord lay not this sin to their charge: and when he had said this he fell asleep" (Acts 7:60).

A good intercessor must be a person of faith, and grounded deeply in the Word of God and love. Faith works by love. David interceded for his nation because he loved God and his people. Love and compassion is the root of intercession. Love demands giving our time, strength, resources finances etc. We cannot intercede for people and hate them at the same time. We must therefore go before God in faith and believe that He is able to give us our desires and needs as well as more than what we ask or think.

David had the intercessor's faith that Jesus described in the gospel. "So Jesus answered and said to them, "Have faith in God.

For assuredly, I say to you, whoever says to this mountain, 'Be removed and be cast into the sea,' and does not doubt in his heart, but believes that those things he says will be done, he will have whatever he says. Therefore I say to you, whatever things you ask when you pray, believe that you receive them, and you will have them. "And whenever you stand praying, if you have anything against anyone, forgive him that your Father in heaven may also forgive you your trespasses" (Mark 11:22-25).

This kind of faith requires love and forgiveness. King David was not easily offended by unresolved issues and had a forgiving heart. David exemplified a forgiving heart when he allowed King Saul to live. Forgiving others releases us from bondages. As intercessors, it is very important that we forgive and love unconditionally.

A good intercessor must be willing to make a sacrifice. It may cost you some extra sleep, time at the dinner table, and additional finances, your dignity, jealousy from loved ones and even your life as you take the baton to be an intercessor. But don't lose heart, stand firm and look to the deliverance of the Lord.

Christ is the hope of glory; He is our hope. King David's hope in God never wavered and our hope in God will also see us through tough situations.

"But I will hope continually, and will yet praise thee more and more. My mouth shall shew forth thy righteousness and thy salvation all the day; for I know not the numbers thereof" (Psalms 71:14-15). Though the author of this Psalm is unknown many believe it was written by King David.

Thou shalt increase my greatness, and comfort me on every side.

159

I will also praise thee with the psaltery, even thy truth, O my God: unto thee will I sing with the harp, O thou Holy One of Israel.

My lips shall greatly rejoice when I sing unto thee; and my soul, which thou hast redeemed.

My tongue also shall talk of thy righteousness all the day-long: for they are confounded, for they are brought unto shame that seek my hurt.

The psalm describes praising God for deliverance. Therefore, you will see the deliverance of God through praise and intercession. God intervenes and delivers when you stand in the gap for others.

God spoke through the Prophet Ezekiel "And I sought for a man among them that should make up the hedge and stand in the gap before me for the land that I should not destroy it, but I found none" (Ezekiel 22:30).

God is always looking for intercessors to rise up and take their posts as watchmen and gatekeepers. God loves all His children and we all have the privilege to come before Him in boldness (Hebrew 4:16).

Some of the benefits Intercession

There are some blessings or benefits for being an intercessor. God promotes people who humble themselves and put others first. Mordecai and Esther interceded with prayer and fasting for the Jews and they were spared from extermination. Mordecai and Esther were promoted by King Ahasuerus (Esther 9:29, 6:11-12, 8:15-17).

The Lord Jesus humbled Himself and died in our place. The Scripture says, "God has given Him a Name that is above every name and at the mention of His Name every knee will bow and every tongue confess" (Philippians 2:9-11).

God grants the intercessors favor. Moses had favor in God's sight that he spoke face to face with God and God revealed His glory to him (Exodus 33:14-23).

God endows intercessors with power and physical strength. He gives the Spirit according to our faith, and since every intercessor has an increasing faith in God, God gives His ever increasing favor and power to those who avail themselves to stand in the gap.

Our Lord Jesus is an intercessor and a warrior, even though He came in as a lamb. He is coming back as a warrior because He is the King of kings and the Captain of Hosts; He is an overcomer!

The Holy Spirit is a warrior. He intercedes for us even when we do not know how to pray. God desires that each of His children be a prayer warrior. Imagine where the devil would be if two thirds of believers were intercessors and prayer warriors.

Let us consider some of the disadvantages of intercession. The devil may attack you directly or attack your loved ones after interceding for others. We should therefore put on the full armor of God as intercessors using every weapon God has given us: the Blood of Jesus, the Word of God, prayers etc. The armor of God is described in the book of Ephesians (Ephesians 6:10-18)   .

The full armor of God is Jesus. The scriptures tells believers to put on Christ daily (Romans 13:14, Gal 3:27). This means we have to arm ourselves with Christ. The armor of God as illustrated in the book of Ephesians are the belt of truth, the breast plate of righteousness, the preparation of the gospel of peace, the shield of faith, the helmet of salvation and the sword of the spirit.

Christ is the "Truth." you have to walk in the truth and avoid lies. Your life is balanced when you speak the truth like David.

Christ is our "Righteousness." You need to remember that and reject every condemnation from the devil. Guard your heart from all evil. David knew the Lord was his righteousness.

Christ is the "Gospel of Peace." Carry Him wherever you go. The more you witness the good news the more you become like Him.

Christ is your "Shield of Faith." He defends you and He is the one every believer hopes for "Hope of glory".

Christ is our "Salvation" (Savior)   You need to protect your mind from all lies about your salvation.

Christ is the "Sword of the Spirit" He is the Word of God .

After putting on Christ you have to stand or persevere, that is the fruit of the Spirit and pray (talk to God) without ceasing.

In relating the armor of God to King David, he knew he was righteous in God's sight, he walked in the truth even when he sinned. He proclaimed God's kingdom among the heathens, and wrote songs about the Kingdom.   He had faith in God and God was his shield.

He knew that God was his salvation as he wrote. "The Lord is my light and my salvation whom shall I fear" Psalm 27:1. He knew the Word of God and carried his sword wherever he went.

The Blood of Jesus is a weapon. Plead the Blood of Jesus over yourselves, your family and all your possessions. We should stand on the promises of God "No weapon forged against us shall prosper" (Isaiah 54:14-17).

Sometimes if you're an intercessor or a prayer warrior you need to take a rest because over working your body makes you vulnerable to the enemy's attack.

Try to live in your anointing. What I mean is that people try to operate on other people's anointing because the devil can really attack you. For instance King Saul asked David to use his armor. David tried it but realized that wouldn't work. If he had used it he might not have killed Goliath. He trusted in God and used what God had given him.

I had a bad experience years ago as an intercessor. I could pray for hours, interceding for others but when I prayed for myself, I would feel a spirit of heaviness. My mind and body would be oppressed so severely that I could hardly focus. I would sometimes see that spirit. It would manifest itself as images of naked beings.

It seemed I wasn't looking through my own eyes. It was like watching a filthy pornographic movie which I have never watched. I knew it was a spiritual attack. It seemed I would get stuck when praying and interceding for others.

I took a step of faith and with effective prayer and fasting God broke all the powers of darkness over my life. I would encourage any reader going through similar opposition to break the powers of darkness with the prayers below, along with your own.

Prayers!

Father God I come to you with a humble spirit. Forgive me for all my sins and the sins and iniquities of my family or others that might have caused my spirit, soul and body to be contaminated. Forgive us of the sins of witchcraft, occult, bestiality, murder, ancestral worship, idol worshipping, etc. Cleanse me with the Blood of Jesus, and make me whole. I renounce any occult, witchcraft, freemasonry, illicit sexual relationship or Lucifer or Satan worship that my family and I have participated in, knowingly or unknowingly. And I confess the Lordship of Christ.

I renounce and break the power of soul ties in my mind, soul, subconscious and every area of my life. I renounce every sin and practice of witchcraft, etc. I break every curse in my life, bloodline and family in Jesus' Name. I cast out every evil spirit out of my life, in Jesus' Name.

Father God release your power, anointing, peace and purity in me. I break every blood covenant with .... (Mention the names of the people that you have had illicit sexual relationship with that you are aware of, every sexual sins in the family that you are aware of.)

I renounce you Satan and your demons. Take your hands off my life because I belong to the Lord Jesus. Heavenly Father, help me and my family to experience your freedom by filling us with Your Spirit so that we can worship you in spirit and in truth. Thank you Father, in Jesus' Name I pray. Amen

It is necessary that we cancel all backlash (spiritual attack) that may come either directly or indirect to us.

The devil might try to attack you directly- physically, financially or in your relationships. He may also try to attack you indirectly through your kids, keeping you busy or numerous distractions.

God is raising up intercessors who will stand in the gap and intercede for His purpose to be fulfilled on the earth. The purpose of God for mankind was that His Son would die in our place to destroy the works of the devil and reconcile us to Him. His desire is that all men would repent and be saved, that none would be lost.

God is knocking at the door of everyone's heart in these end times. He wants those who are available; who will say "Lord here am I, send me" just as the Prophet Isaiah said.

How many of us have put a note at the door of our heart "DO NOT DISTURB?"

How many of us have answered "Yes", but are still procrastinating, finding excuses, or filled with fear, insecurity, doubt or double mindedness; like the man who wanted to go and bid farewell to his family when the Lord Jesus called him to follow Him?

"And another also said Lord, I will follow thee, but let me first go bid them farewell, which are at home at my house. And Jesus said unto him. No man having put his hands to the plough and looking back is fit for the Kingdom of God" (Luke 9:6).

I will tell a bit of my story. It has been my passion and mission to minister to people all over the world but first of all to my family back in Ghana. My prayer several years was "Lord, send me." Then in 2010 the Lord told me to move from Illinois to Los Angeles, California. It was a struggle for me. I didn't know anyone in California neither did I know California except on the map.

Moreover there was an economic recession. California had one of the highest states of unemployment and I had not saved the needed funds for making the move.

I made several trips to California, before I finally moved. I was on vacation when I made my final trip. I was tempted to go back to Chicago when my vacation was almost over. I thought throughout the night and early morning but I heard in my right ear, "you cannot put your hands on a plough and look back." I knew that was the Lord so I obeyed Him and stayed in California and just live by faith! (Just trust God for daily provision). I stopped that praying (Lord me send) for a while.

Maybe you have a similar story like me, know that God is preparing you for something great! Don't give up. Hold fast to the promises of God. You are a part of God's army.

We have to be ready to fight the good fight of faith like King David. He was always ready to intercede or wage war on behalf of his nation. He was always keen to seek the direction of God.

I pray that God would let you hear His voice even as He has commissioned you and I to bring the lost into His Kingdom. The Psalmist (likely David) wrote "Ask of me and I will give thee the heathen for thine inheritance and uttermost parts of the earth for thy possessions" (Psalm 2: 8).

As we seek God's face in prayer, He will give us the nations of the earth through effective evangelism; through our love. As we help the poor widows, orphans, homeless, victims of human and sex trafficking and building Churches in remote places of the earth.

If our Lord is a warrior, and He said "the violent takes it by for force", then I suggest to you that the Church has to be hot and not cold or lukewarm. God will defend and protect our backs when we put on the full armor of God and stay in prayer!

After all, Christians are not called to passivity. Being cold is being passive. God wants his children to be hot like King David. We are even more than conquerors because of Christ. "Nothing can separate you from the love of God through Christ" (Romans 8:37-39). God will subdue your enemies under your feet.

God is looking for someone who will stand in the gap for others. Would you be the one?

Personal Notes.

Mother Theresa is a role model like King David.
Selflessness is Love centered.

Chapter 8.

Living a selfless Life-Love centered Living!

Selfishness is common in every society. People think of themselves as more important than others and are careless about how their actions affect the people around them.

The world we live in is "ME, ME" oriented. It's the root of a dysfunctional society. What is a selfless life? It is living a life where we put others first. We seek the interest or the common good of others. It is living a sacrificial life and ready to place others first. It is therefore not self-promoting but self-denying. David was a self-less man in many ways. He loved his neighbors and the people around him and was willing to share with others. Does this sound like you?

In one of the familiar stories about him and his mighty men of war, we read how he defeated his enemies at Ziklag with the help of a few of his men. Though those who went to war with him were self-centered, David listened to his heart and shared the booty with the rest who couldn't go because they were feeble. David was gracious and loving because he valued his relationship with those men (1Samuel 30:21-30, 2 Sam 23:13-17).

Selfishness is like a toxic that is breaking up a lot of relationships: both marital and otherwise, while selflessness is that strong element that builds the relationship. Living a selfless life does not come automatic, but it's something we most purpose in our hearts to do. The more we do the more mature we become.

Selflessness is a gain but selfishness is a sin that can cause us to put all people behind us not excluding God because it causes people to see themselves more important than others.

We see it in the nations, especially in the developing countries. Most of the leaders that come into power monopolize almost everything and do not care about the wellbeing or welfare of the citizens. The results are obvious as we see and hear through the media, etc. Some live very luxuriously while most of the citizens really suffer: physically, emotionally, psychologically and financially because most of the people can hardly afford a balanced diet meal for themselves and their families.

However, over the centuries God has been sending missionaries to the nations—especially those that are oppressed—with the good news. Mother Theresa was a model of someone who lived a selfless life like King David.

Most of the chaos and upsurges are because the people can no longer take the oppression and try to oust the President or the leaders if possible. Chaos is the absence of selflessness.

Adults can be more selfish compared to kids though there are some are equally like adults. Some kids are independent because they do not have siblings. They have all their toys and stuff to themselves. Possibly, they share only when they go to school. And some even find it hard to play or share with others since they are mostly independent.

We find selfishness everywhere in the society. It's found in our homes, neighborhoods, schools, business, cooperation and private sectors. We see it in our governments, sports, entertainment, and everywhere even in the body of Christ.

We see some people with certain positions or gifted being selfish. I have noticed that the moment I share something with others, being food or even about some of the revelation knowledge God has given me, I feel relieved. It's like a burden has been lifted off me. It's good to have the attitude of sharing.

Self-centeredness is therefore the fruit of the flesh. But people who are selfless do not try or pretend to be self-righteous. They certainly see themselves vulnerable.

King David was not self-righteous, in fact we read from the book of Psalms (Psalms 32 & 51). How he was opened before God because he knew that his sins were naked before God. He admitted and acknowledged his sins instead of hiding them.

The Scripture says we are saved by the grace of God not by our works so this should always remind us that our righteousness can never please God; they are like filthy rags before God.

Love is the root of selflessness. You can't be selfless if you don't love. Love will cause you to put others before yourself. God is love and Christ is the love of God and love does not boast or exalt itself. The Lord Jesus certainly demonstrated the selfless love of God in various scenarios.

For instance a lady being caught in committing adultery, who according to the law should be stoned, was forgiven and counseled by the Lord to sin no more (John 8:1-11)!

Putting others before yourself would definitely cause you to be on your knees or to be humbled. You will love the unlovable. It is easy to love those who love you right? What about those who hate you, those who gossip about you or those who want your downfall?

It is absolutely hard to do that in our own strength however, with God all things are possible since His Spirit will help us in our weaknesses.

Look at the love King David had for King Saul in spite of all the plans to destroy David. God gave him the grace to love King Saul. You can also do that by the grace of God. Glory to God!

Love is the motivational ingredient that drives us to live a selfless life. We will love our neighbors as ourselves when the love of God is at work in us. Every decision or words that we utter to someone we will first put ourselves in their situations and feel how it looks like to be in their shoes.

Here comes the golden rule. "So in everything, do to others what you would have them do to you, for this sums up the Law and the Prophets" (Matthew 7:12).

We read in the Scriptures the story of David and three of his mighty men (2 Samuel 23:8-39). Those men overheard David saying how he longed to get a drink from the well in Bethlehem. David of course was from Bethlehem but he was at war with the Philistines at that time in order to get to Bethlehem, they had to go through the garrison of the Philistines.

Those three mighty men risked their life and went through their enemy's camp without David's knowledge to get him the water. David refused to drink the water when the men brought it. This shows the kind of person David was. He poured the water before the Lord as a sign of humility and innocence of the blood of those men who risked their life for his sake. They could have lost their lives in doing that and he did not want to encourage any of them to take such risk again. See how selfless he was.

He didn't want to take advantage of others. That was the fruit of humility. Humbleness causes us to be selfless. As I wrote in the first chapter about how King David was humble (2 Samuel 23:3-7). I'm wondering how many of us will love others and be loyal to them even when it hurts.

There was a time when I was really discouraged and lost interest in interceding effectively for my spiritual leaders. This was because I was in a ministry and I used to fast and pray for the leadership most of the time. I realized that I was even spending more time in praying for them than for my family. Though I did pray for my family, I guess my priority was seeing the power of God being manifested at the Church.

There was a split in the Church from the leadership through the entire congregation. I decided to pray effectively for my family more than I had ever done. I did not want to pray any longer for the leadership of the new Church that I had joined like I did before but the Holy Spirit convicted me after a while. I then decided to pray for the Church.

God healed me and brought me to the right perspective of seeing the need to intercede both for my family and for the Church. Some of my family members were saved during that time and I was able to intercede for my new Pastor, the leadership, and the various ministries in the Church, as well as the entire congregation of the new Church.

Why am I saying this? Because of the need for being loyal and faithful to our leaders, the people God has placed over our life whether at our jobs, home, etc.

Living a selfless life takes us back to "Agape Love," God's unconditional love for us. It is the same love that He wants us to show to our neighbors. Our Lord simplified it by summarizing all the laws into two "Love the LORD your God with all your heart and with all your soul and with all your mind. This is the first and greatest commandment. And the second is like it: Love your neighbor as yourself. All the law and the Prophets hang on these commandments" (Matthew 22:37-40, NIV).

I think every believer should memorize and meditate on the love chapter in the Bible. This popular scripture on love (1Corinthians 13) tells us that love is not self-seeking.

1 Corinthian 13

"Though I speak with the tongues of men and of angels, but have not love, I have become sounding brass or a clanging cymbal. And though I have the gift of prophecy, and understand all mysteries and all knowledge, and though I have all faith, so that I could remove mountains, but have not love, I am nothing. And though I bestow all my goods to feed the poor, and though I give my body to be burned, but have not love, it profits me nothing.

Love suffers long and is kind; love does not envy; love does not parade itself, is not puffed up; does not behave rudely, does not seek its own, is not provoked, thinks no evil; does not rejoice in iniquity, but rejoices in the truth; bears all things, believes all things, hopes all things, endures all things.

Love never fails. But whether there are prophecies, they will fail; whether there are tongues, they will cease; whether there is knowledge, it will vanish away. For we know in part and we prophesy in part. But when that which is perfect has come, then that which is in part will be done away.

When I was a child, I spoke as a child, I understood as a child, I thought as a child; but when I became a man, I put away childish *things*. For now we see in a mirror, dimly, but then face to face. Now I know in part, but then I shall know just as I also am known.

And now abide faith, hope, love, these three; but the greatest of these is love."

I am quite sure if we all truly understand it and actually put these into practice the earth would be a lovely place to live in.

The Holy Spirit is our Guide and Counselor who guides us into all truth. It is really bad to see some believers taking advantage of others. I believe most of us might have been victimized before.

How do we use our positions to influence others? Is it controlling and manipulating or loving?

Selfishness may dominate someone as a result of pride but a person can be selfless because of humility. Pride is probably the major reason why some people take advantage of others. Selfless people don't misuse or take advantage of others.

Some people want others to see that they are anointed or the favor of God is on them. Some of the reasons why people may take advantage of others may be gender, racial, language, nationality differences.

It is easy to find ourselves caught-up trying to take advantage of others but the moment we come to our senses or get convicted by the Holy Spirit we must repent and do the right thing. Accepting our faults cause us to humble ourselves but it is all good because then we can walk in God's grace.

I like what John the Baptist told the Jews who were wondering who he was. John the Baptist started his ministry as a Prophet after the silent period or dark ages. This was a period of about four hundred years that the Israelites did not hear from God because there was no Prophet during all those period. Then suddenly John the Baptist appeared, dressed in camel leather and calling the people to repentance.

He was confronted by the Pharisees, the Scribes and all the sects about his identity, because Israel was desperately expecting the Messiah to deliver them from the Roman Empire. He was very transparent and secured about his position as a forerunner. He told those who had come to him for counseling to do no violence to any man, neither accuse any one falsely (Luke 3:14).

Most of those people were soldiers who were taking bribes from the rich people and perverting justice. The poor and innocent were the victims

God wants us to love our neighbors as ourselves irrespective of their race, ethnicity, genders, educational background, appearance, etc. He is no respecter of persons and He wants us to be like Him.

King David was loyal and kept his word even when it hurt to speak the truth or to do the right thing. He was really secure in his relationship with God even though there were some instances one can say he was depressed, yet he knew God was stronger than what he was going through. At the end of most of his songs he expressed his trust in God.

He trusted God to see him through every circumstance. For instance, some of the songs that showed that he was depressed are Psalms 32, 38, 51. He shared his heart openly without keeping it secret.

It is very easy to be tempted in this hectic and busy world we now live in. The worldly system is running at a faster rate than you can imagine and making it sometimes hard for one to recognize the needs of the people around us.

However, at the same time God wants His children to be mindful of His Word. People are becoming more and more lovers of themselves. He wants us to love like He does.

Is it easy to love God and others like the way God requires us? Absolutely Not! Love does not come automatically when we get saved. We need to make the choice and work on that daily by practicing what the Word says. We do that by reading the Word of God and asking God to show us how to love.

Sometime people use drugs, alcohol etc because of selfishness. They don't love themselves and the people around them. And they really don't care about the damage they cause to others through their decisions. They believe no one loves them, but that is one of the major lies of the devil. May God set such people free for them to know the true?

King David knew the value of life in the sight of God as most of us know; or acknowledge that fact.

"Owe no man anything, but to love one another: for he that loveth another hath fulfilled the Law" (Romans 13:8, KJV).

Personal Notes.

| |
| |
| |
| |
| |
| |
| |
| |
| |
| |

God loves a cheerful giver. Givers never lose!

Chapter 9

Joyful Giver

Givers Never Lack!

Giving could be an interesting but controversial subject, especially when it comes to giving to a Church or non-profit organization. Some people get offended when you talk about giving, but others may get excited because they believe in giving. In either case, giving and receiving is a principle in the Kingdom of God because the Word of God says "give and it shall be given to you," and "it is more blessed to give than to receive" (Luke 6:38, Acts 20:35).

The principle can be compared to a farmer. When a farmer sows, he expects a harvest in proportion to whatever was sown. Even though this principle is true some people abuse the Word of God and take advantage of others quite often. This has brought a lot of misunderstanding and misconceptions about giving in the Body of Christ.

Another thought about why King David was a giver could be the fact that he knew that God created all things. God has entrusted man with all but at the same time man is responsible to give it all back to God in serving Him and others.

"Look, the highest heavens and the earth and everything in it all belong to the LORD your God" (Deuteronomy 10:14).

When we receive from God freely, we should give freely. But sometimes people think they have what they have because of their own achievement. It is absolutely wrong. God gives us the power to be wealthy (Deuteronomy 8:18).

There are several motives people have for giving. Some give to the needy people around them or to non-profit organizations just to be taxed less. That's kind of like giving to oneself.

Others give because they actually love the poor and needy and have compassion on them. Some people give because they have abundance. Some may give because they are givers or they get motivated when they see others giving. In which category do you find yourself?

Do you give freely or grudgingly? Are you a taker or a giver? Well, I pray God will touch our hearts as we discuss this topic and give grace to each one who struggles with giving so that giving freely would not be a big issue for you whether you are giving to an individual or collectively.

God is the greatest giver, AMEN! The nature of God is to give and even much more than we ask or think according to His power in us. He even gives to sinners what they want out of His mercy and sovereignty. How much more will He not give to those who diligently seek Him!

There are so many Scriptures that confirm the fact that God is a generous giver. One of the most famous scriptures usually quoted by many people—both believers and unbelievers—talks about God giving to the world because of love.

"For God so loved the world that He gave His only begotten Son, that whoever believes in Him should not perish but have an everlasting life" (John 3:16).

God gave His Son to the world because He loved the world. The world in the Greek language is "kosmos" or "cosmos" in English. It refers to the universe... typically mankind, which means God loves all men and desire that all men would be saved, that was why He gave us the greatest gift ever given to mankind, the Lord Jesus Christ.

Therefore since God is the greatest giver, I can say it would be absurd for God to declare that David was a man after His heart if King David was a stingy person.

King David was a generous giver. He gave not only to God but also to individuals. He gave his life to the Israelites, he gave his financial resources etc. to the advancement of God's Kingdom. He was someone who purposed in his heart to give the best to God.

One thing you should take note of is that giving is a gift. The Bible tells us that some have been given the gift of giving (Romans 12:6-8). Even though the gifts of the spirit are mentioned in the New Testament, people in the Old Testament knew about the Holy Spirit through the intuition or prompting they sensed. Secondly

180

the nature of God in man causes people to give even if they are not believers, therefore all believers should be givers to some extent.

For instance, my dad was a giver before he accepted the Lord. He was a young flight sergeant in the Royal Air force in Gold Coast (Ghana). He was going to the Air-force base one day for a flight to one of the African countries during the second world war. He was delayed by a beggar who held him fast that he couldn't move and told him to wait because he has something important to tell him. He was delayed by this beggar so they took off without him.

The plane crashed killing all of them. He was single and no children at that time. As I was growing up my siblings and I would watch my dad stopping by the street every morning to give money to beggars before going to work. He was a real giver. I can't talk about giving without mentioning my father Edward Osei-Bonsu's name. He sponsored several children to further their education throughout his entire life.

When we give we receive. We may not be rewarded in the very thing we give but in something else. For instance, we see in the Scriptures different people who gave to strangers or Angels like Abraham gave food, shelter etc. to the three men (Genesis 18), and King David gave food to a starving Ethiopian (1Samuel 30). In both of these stories there were good rewards for their giving. (Also I believe it was an angel who hindered my father from boarding the plane). God hasn't changed. He can still do what He did for Abraham for you and I as we give even to strangers.

Even though giving was part of the culture, in the Bible days there were people like King David who had the gift of giving. That's probably why Abigail's husband Nabal seemed strange to him (1 Samuel 25).

We will study a couple of things that King David did for God and the nation of Israel in terms of giving in this chapter.

Quite a lot of people in the Bible were givers in some way, but the generosity of King David tops it all. He loved God so much that he wanted to build a house for God. King David gave tremendously towards the building of the temple which even motivated the Israelites to imitate him (1 Chronicles 29:16-17).

Love goes with giving. We can give our time, our finances, resources, or inheritance to someone when we love that person. Love compels us to give like Amy Carmichael, a missionary to India said, "You can give without loving, but you cannot *love* without giving."

God is love and love is God. If anyone loves God that person will truly give from the heart because the Spirit of God does the prompting. The person does not give up so easily because love does not easily give up.

We reap love when we sow love though sometimes it doesn't work that way. A farmer's harvest can be determined by when, what, and where he sows. There is seed time and harvest.

These are kairos and kronos times (explained in chapter 3). Sowing at the right time in the natural brings a bountiful harvest just as investing in God's kingdom in the Kairos time will also bring a great supernatural harvest. Where we sow will determine our harvest. For instance when you sow on stony ground, the probability of having a scanty harvest is inevitable. However,

182

when you sow on a fertile ground, there would be a bountiful harvest.

Therefore the place we choose to invest our time, finances, talents, etc, is important. It is always good to discern like King David and invest in God's Kingdom at the right time. He knew that the perfect time to build a house for God was after God had given Israel rest from most of the strong nations around them.

Giving is not only about finances. It is also about our time, our resources, our talents, spiritual gifting, etc. Where you give is actually the destination of the ministries or individuals you invest in.

For instance, if you donate money to ministries or organizations that support abortion you need to know that you are helping those organizations to kill. And I don't think God can truly bless you for doing that.

All these principles are true for both natural and spiritual sowing. Spiritual seeds are mainly our finances, resources, time etc. You will reap bountifully when you invest in God's Kingdom like King David did. He was Kingdom minded. He sought the Kingdom and its righteousness first (Matthew 6:33). He knew he could not out-give God. He knew his God who had brought him from the shepherds fold to kingship. He never despised his humble beginnings so he was able to entrust God with his entire life.

King David did not want to give cheap things to God. He acknowledged God as King. You do not go to the King with empty hands or things that are not of good quality. If you go before the King with a gift from your heart you receive favor from him. Let me ask you, do you give God the best part of your time? There are some people who never give but instead are always expecting. I doubt they will meet their expectations.

There was a plague in Israel that resulted in the death of about seventy thousand people over night. The cause of it was that King David counted his army without the instructions of God. He probably was getting ready for war or perhaps he just arrogantly did it against better knowledge.

He wanted to build an altar for God because of that calamity. He therefore sought to buy a threshing floor to build an altar of sacrifice to God, (threshing floors were floors used to separate the grain from the chaff at harvest times). He had a free offer from the owner of the land but he refused to take it, just as he refused to drink the water that his mighty men fetched him from Bethlehem.

"Then the king said to Araunah, 'No, but I will surely buy it from you for a price; nor will I offer burnt offerings to the LORD my God with that which costs me nothing.' So David bought the threshing floor and the oxen for fifty shekels of silver. And David built there an altar to the LORD, and offered burnt offerings and peace offerings. So the LORD heeded the prayers for the land, and the plague was withdrawn from Israel" (2 Samuel 24:24-25).

God is love and His Son is the Love of God. The Lord Jesus in summarizing the laws into two said, "Thou shall love the Lord thy God with all thy heart and with all thy soul and with all thy mind" (Matthew 22:37).

We cannot say we love God and give Him our leftovers. King David gave generously and cheerfully. Generous givers are always cheerful, because givers never loose. It is an investment. It is not like the stock market where people get panic and heart attacks because of the uncertainty of the world market; this is a secure investment. We do not get our reward only in Heaven, but also here on earth (Luke 6:38, Mark 10:29-30).

God wants us to love and give cheerfully to His Kingdom. He gives us over and above what we deserve if we obey Him. He wants us to give even to our enemies when they are hungry without any grudge. It is easy to give to those who love you or those whom we love. God causes the sun to shine on the righteous and the wicked. He wants us to be like Him.

The Apostle Paul said it right in the love chapter (1 Corinthians 13), that if we give all of our possessions to the poor and after that offer our bodies to be burned, but have no love, we have gained nothing.

We must always give with love and when we give we should expect rewards from God, but not from the people we give to or from mankind in general. God is our reward; our source of supply, and NOT man. We will be disappointed if we expect the reward from man. God said cursed is any man who trusts in man, so we trust in God and not in man (Jeremiah 17:5-6). Wives should even trust in God as their source of provision and not their husbands.

God watches us when we give like the Lord watched the people as they gave. Just as He commented on the widow's offering of two pennies I believe God is keeping record of all our giving (Mark 12: 41-44). Paul wrote how the Philippian church gave out of their poverty, for they were the only church that sent a gift to Paul during his imprisonment.

185

Paul's heart was full of joy and he blessed them with his prayer that God would supply all their needs according to His riches and glory in Christ Jesus (Philippians 4:19).

Sometimes when we give, we believe God for corresponding blessings (harvest), possibly within a few days or a couple of days afterward. We sometimes get disappointed and frustrated when we do not receive any thing for a while.

Just as some seeds take long to germinate and bear fruit, so some investments in the Kingdom take a while to bring in the returns. It is so with businesses. Sometimes we have to learn how to wait on God for our reward like King David wrote (Psalm 27:14).

It could be a long or short duration, but wait because it is part of life and part of the journey. However, you never lose when you invest in God's kingdom. King David invested in the Kingdom with his life by fighting for the Israelites, with his finances, time etc. He believed in generational blessings, that whatever he had invested would be passed on to his generation and also to the nation as a whole because God would bless the righteous even to a thousand generations (Exodus 20:6).

Many of us have been disappointed a couple of times because we sowed and we had nothing in return even though we gave to advance the Kingdom of God. Some too may have been disappointed because they realized they gave to the wrong organization or individuals. Or possibly you were in a Church and they were building a house for God and you donated from your house but the funds have been misused or whatever.

The best thing is to forgive yourself and let God judge and also let Him lead you the next time with your giving. Be careful to discern between the spirit and emotions.

Maybe you have a testimony like mine and you do not want to invest in the Kingdom of God any longer. You know what? That's fine. Maybe you need a time to grieve. However, when you hear God's voice it's better to obey than to sacrifice.

I went through a series of trials some years back and I was somehow discouraged to give wholeheartedly to Churches and ministries. In 2003 I paid $300 to my local Church as part of my pledge for a building fund on a Sunday, the day before Labor Day. The next day which was Labor Day, I went to a conference and paid $300 to support a Ministry that reached out to the Jews in Israel.

On my way home I had an accident and unfortunately my insurance expired on that Labor Day. I remembered it while I was in the conference room, and decided to renew the next morning. On my way home I hit someone's car. It was a long story full of trials for me.

I was initially confused when I went through all those trials, but I knew God was in control and He would bring me out of those tests. He brought me out after a while and because He has given me the gift of giving, I started giving again.

Having a Kingdom mindset will bring us to the right posture like King David. A Kingdom mindset is thinking like a royalty. You are royalty if you believe in Christ. Royalties know how to receive gifts and know how to give gifts. In their hearts and minds it's all about advancing or building the Kingdom.

God's favor and protection was on David from his childhood as he gave his life, talents, finances, etc to God and his fellow men: killing Goliath, serving King Saul, destroying nations and kings, giving towards the building of the Temple, etc.

David trusted in God despite all he went through. He did not even entrust himself in his warriors, though he had mighty warriors who were always ready to fight for him.

David remembered how God had protected him from the wilderness, through the caves, and brought him to the palace. Any ungrateful person hates the words, "Thank you." David was always grateful and thankful to God; praising and worshipping Him all the time. It is no wonder God he won God's heart. He wrote:

"The LORD is my light and my salvation;
Whom shall I fear?
The LORD is the strength of my life;
Of whom shall I be afraid?
When the wicked came against me
To eat up my flesh,
My enemies and foes,
They stumbled and fell.
Though an army may encamp against me,
My heart shall not fear;
Though war may rise against me,
In this I will be confident.
One thing I have desired of the LORD,

That will I seek:
That I may dwell in the house of the LORD
All the days of my life,
To behold the beauty of the LORD,
And to inquire in His temple.
For in the time of trouble
He shall hide me in His pavilion;
And now my head shall be lifted up above my enemies all around
me;
Therefore I will offer sacrifices of joy in His tabernacle;
I will sing, yes, I will sing praises to the LORD.
Hear, O LORD, when I cry with my voice!
Have mercy also upon me, and answer me.
When You said, "Seek My face,"
My heart said to You, "Your face, LORD, I will seek."
Do not hide Your face from me;
Do not turn Your servant away in anger;
You have been my help;
Do not leave me nor forsake me,
O God of my salvation.
When my father and my mother forsake me,
Then the LORD will take care of me.
Teach me Your way, O LORD,
And lead me in a smooth path, because of my enemies.
Do not deliver me to the will of my adversaries;
For false witnesses have risen against me,
And such as breathe out violence. I would have lost heart, unless I
had believed
That I would see the goodness of the LORD   In the land of the
living.

Wait on the LORD;
Be of good courage,
And He shall strengthen your heart;
Wait, I say, on the LORD!" (Psalm 27)

David trusted God for complete provision, protection, etc.
Sometimes I feel it is harder for most people in the western world to grasp the concept of trusting God wholeheartedly for everything, including the next meal... than for those in the developing countries. People in developing nations understand how it is to depend on God's daily provision. Most of the people in the developed countries may have many avenues of support. For instance in the U.S. and most European countries, people have access to government support while the people in the developing countries do not have those privileges.

They do not think about tomorrow. They only think about what to eat today. It is enough for most of them. They believe in the Scriptures and walk in it. The Lord Jesus taught us not to be anxious about tomorrow. "Therefore I tell you, do not worry about your life, what you will eat or drink; or about your body, what you will wear. Is not your life more than food and your body more than clothes (Matthew 6:25)?

King David honored God and he knew how to offer a living sacrifice to God. That was why he told Araunah the Jebusite that he would not sacrifice anything to God that would not cost him something. Like God told Moses to tell the Israelites not to bring sick or deformed animals for sacrifice. They were supposed to sacrifice the first fruits of their crops to God. The first fruits were strong and healthy.

God honored David because David honored God, "Therefore, the LORD, the God of Israel, says: I promised that your branch of the tribe of Levi would always be my priests. "I will honor those who honor me, and I will despise those who think lightly of me" (1 Samuel 2:30).

In the book of Romans we read that we should give or offer ourselves as a living sacrifice, holy and acceptable unto God, for that is our reasonable act of worship (Romans 12:1-2). When you sacrifice something to God it doesn't belong to you any longer. Whatever you do or give to God must come from a pure heart. Likewise, whatever you do or give to others must come from your heart and you must do it as if you were doing it for the Lord (Ephesians 6:7, Colossians 3: 23).

David purposed it in his heart and mind to love God and give all his best to God because he honored God, he loved Him, and he had a Kingdom mindset. And he gave for with the right attitude and motive.

In conclusion, it is more blessed to give than to receive because no one can out- give God, however we should be led by the Spirit and not emotions! Giving and receiving is a principle in the Kingdom of God. Give with a purpose and for the right motive!

Personal Notes.

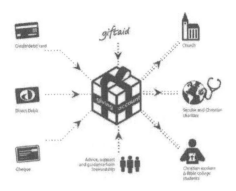

Kingdom mindset- Every King wants His Kingdom to advance. God has a reward for the faithful servants

Chapter 10

A Faithful Steward and an Administrator.

King David was a good administrator.   Administration is one of the spiritual gifts according to the Scriptures.   The gift of administration is the God-given ability to give direction and make decisions on behalf of others that results in an efficient operation and accomplishment of goals. Administration includes the ability to organize people, things information, finances etc.

"Now you are the body of Christ, and members individually. And God has appointed these in the church: first apostles, second prophets, third teachers, after that miracles, then gift's of healings, helps, administrating and various kinds of tongues" (1 Corinthians 12:27-28).

Even though this gift is listed along with other gifts in the New Testament, people like Joseph in the Old Testament who became a Prime Minster in Egypt had that gift of administration.

There are of course people who are good administrators through book knowledge, but that is not what we are talking about right now, even though those people play an important role in building and advancing our businesses and overall economy.

I believe David's gift of administration might have been developed in his early age when he was a shepherd. Even though the Scripture does not state how old he was when he began to shepherd his father's flock. It is possible he might have started at a very tender age before Samuel anointed him because in the Jewish culture the younger boy in the family was the shepherd. The oldest starts and then hands over to the next oldest so eventually the youngest would have a long way to go (1Samuel16:13).

Being experienced in shepherding a flock gave him more advantage in mobilizing and administrating his men of war (mighty men) and ruling over the tribe of Judah then the nation of Israel. He was a hard worker and a consistent person. He knew how to prioritize his time by waking up early in the morning to seek the face of God.

For instance, this was a song written by King David when he was in the Judean wilderness when his son Absalom dethroned him. "O *God*, you are my will I seek you: my soul thirsts for you, my flesh longs for you in a dry and God; early thirsty land" (Psalm 63:1). He had the wisdom to spend time alone with God early in the morning before anything else. Some of wake up longing for a Starbucks coffee before thanking the Lord

The Solomon's Temple.

His preparation towards the building of the temple was fabulous and really well organized (1Chronicles 22-27). Can you image how he wanted the architectural, the spiritual atmosphere, the whole set up and how the building had to be maintained? Some people have only a small house but they cannot maintain it. This is the summary of the things he did in his preparation for the Temple which his son Solomon then built.

He arranged for the building itself, the altar as well as the necessary furnishings needed for the Temple. He assigned duties to the Levites, he divided the priests into groups, and he assigned the musicians their tasks. The musicians were to sing, the Temple guards were the security, the duties of other officials, commanders of the army, and the officers of the tribes are also detailed according to the scriptures (1 Chronicles 22-27).

Each department had their specific role to play. Every department was to be in operation daily on a 24/7 basis, except for the High Priest who was to go into the Holy of Holies once a year on the day of atonement when he would go to atone by covering the mercy seat of the Ark of the Covenant with the blood of goats, bullocks, etc.

I had a little glimpse of how things are well-organized in Heaven after reading those scriptures about David's preparation for the Temple.

It was similar to how the tabernacle and Ark of the Covenant were built by Moses. God specifically instructed Moses giving him the exact measurements and the materials it was to be built with (Exodus 31, 37).

I believe God wants us to know the order of worship and service; doing things in the right order and by protocol here on earth, that was why the Lord Jesus taught us how to pray, "Your kingdom come, Your will be done on earth as it is in Heaven" (Matthew 6:10).

We serve a God of order and Excellency, and even though not all of us have the gift of administration like David or Joseph we should know how to be organized to some extent. So we can desire for the gift of administration if we want but with good motives. How can we overcome our enemy the devil if we do not really know how to be organized or structured?

The devil has schemes. Schemes are a large-scale systematic plan or arrangement for obtaining some particular object or putting a particular idea into effect. The schemes of the devil are evil; to steal, kill and destroy (John 10:10). That is why God expects His children to be good planners like the ant.

"Go to the ant, you sluggard; consider its ways and be wise! It has no commander, no overseer or ruler, yet it stores its provisions in summer and gathers its food at harvest. How long will you lie there, you sluggard? When will you get up from your sleep? A little sleep, a little slumber, a little folding of the hands to rest and poverty will come on you like a bandit and scarcity like an armed man" (Proverbs 6:6-11).

King David's gift of administration helped him to set achievable goals, in training his warriors, planning wars, and constantly destroying his enemies. He had the gift of administration of course, and he was guided by the Spirit of God, however I think he was a God's chaser. This is something you and I can learn from.

The Apostle Paul was right when he wrote, "Let all things be done decently and orderly." God wants all that we do in the Kingdom to be organized and planned well primarily by the Holy Spirit. The Spirit of God is an Administrator.

When God created the world and it was formless, the Spirit of God was hovering over the waters and the waters separated from the lands (Genesis 1, the account of creation). He was present during creation. Therefore when we commit things into His hands He will align them rightly.

David knew how to strategize for every assignment that needed to be executed by him. It is no surprise that God said David was a man after His own heart. Do you see yourself as a man or woman after God's own heart? With faith he overlooked all those limitations in life and decided to prepare all that his son Solomon would need in building the temple.

David chose people who were skilled and competent in fulfilling the positions he had placed them in. He knew God is an extravagant God. He is a God of plans and purposes, and designs that everything pertaining to His Kingdom must be done with excellence.

How do you choose your employees? Sometimes we may choose people with little potential and that may not necessarily have the particular requirements we want. That's fine, but choosing skillfully can save our time and finances in so many ways. People who want to maximize their potential!

People who are talented or have learned to be administrators but are unbelievers could be more skillful when they accept the Lord because then the Holy Spirit would come into them when they get saved. The Holy Spirit takes absolute control over their talents and molds them completely into new people so that they are more effective than before and bring glory to God through their gifts and talents.

There is a difference between a gift and a talent. A talent is a natural skill or special ability that allows someone to do something well. A gift of the Spirit is a special grace to an individual by God for them to operate in ways which are beyond their natural capability. The purpose of God giving the gift to the individual is to build others up through that gift.

I pray God will raise more believers in the business sectors all across the globe. People with kingdom mindsets and the kind of anointing Joseph had so that they would do business in God's ways and take dominion over the marketplace for the sake of the Kingdom. And the kind of kingly anointing that was on David would be released on believers now Amen!

People with the gift of administration are more musical like King David. I read the book about personality profiles by Florence Littauer years back and I understand from the writer that there are four personalities. Well, there could be even more. However, I am interested in how she described the melancholy profile–they are people who are well organized. They are musical. Most often writers or poets are good administrators.

We see a bit of God's nature (though one could see God's nature in all the personalities because we all have a little bit of God's DNA). People of such a personality profile are "detailed." I personally believe that almost all the writers of the Bible had that personality since they were always careful in their expressions.

King David was a good planner and a good steward. We have to be good planners and managers of whatever God has entrusted to us. This includes our finances, time, resources, relationships, etc.

A steward is someone whose job is to manage the land and property of another. King David knew that he was a steward over all that God had entrusted him with.

I think faithfulness and loyalty are the basic ingredients we need to have if we want to increase in life or to flow in the full gifts and talents God has given us. Also if we want God to give us our own gifts, we desperately need to be faithful and loyal.

There are some people who are looking for more money now, but guess what… if they were to get it their lives would be ruined by the money. Money will tell them where to go and what to do instead of them telling the money what services they need.

King David accomplished one of his goals by bringing the Ark of the Covenant back to Israel after being captured by the Philistines (2 Samuel 5:25, 2 Samuel 6:1:2, 17:18) His desire was to maintain their heritage by bringing the nation under One God; the God of their forefathers. History is very important and it's precious to the Jews because God asked them to pass the legacy of their heritage on to the next generation and each successive one after.

King David had a servant's heart. His main objective was to serve his master first, and then others next. King David took good care of his father's sheep as a young man. He did not allow any ferocious animals to kill any of the sheep even though they were not his personal possession. He could have cared less about the sheep when they were in danger, after all he was not the oldest son in the family to inherit his father possessions, yet he protected them with his whole heart and life.

David's words to King Saul just before he fought with Goliath: "David said unto Saul, thy servant kept his father's sheep, and there came a lion and a bear and took a lamb out of the flock, and I went out after him and smote him and delivered it out of his mouth and when he arose against me, I caught him by the his beard, and smote him and slew him. Thy servant slew both a lion and the bear and this uncircumcised Philistine shall be as one of them" (1 Samuel 17:34).

I am quite sure King Saul was wondering how this little fellow slew those wild animals. Aren't you afraid of King David? He understood the fact that a servant is not above his master neither a student above his teacher. He was faithful with the little God gave to him, even with his father's flock. So God gave him more (the nation of Israel) to rule over.

199

The Scripture tells us that our gifts will make room for us and will bring us before great men (Proverbs 18:16). We can offer gifts to people that could bring us before great men but we have to give with the right motive. David's servant heart and gifts brought him before King Saul (1 Samuel 16:18), and even the King of the Philistines, who was the enemy of Israel (1 Samuel 27).

"And Saul's servants said unto him, behold now, an evil spirit from God troubleth thee. Let our lord now command thy servants, which are before thee, to seek out a man, who is a cunning player on an harp: and it shall come to pass, when the evil spirit from God is upon thee, that he shall play with his hand, and thou shalt be well. And Saul said unto his servants, Provide me now a man that can play well, and bring him to me.

Then answered one of the servants, and said, Behold, I have seen a son of Jesse the Bethlehemite, that is cunning in playing, and a mighty valiant man, and a man of war, and prudent in matters, and a comely person, and the LORD is with him.

Wherefore Saul sent messengers unto Jesse, and said, Send me David thy son, which is with the sheep. And Jesse took an ass laden with bread, and a bottle of wine, and a kid, and sent them by David his son unto Saul.

And David came to Saul, and stood before him: and he loved him greatly; and he became his armour bearer. And Saul sent to Jesse, saying, Let David, I pray thee, stand before me; for he hath found favour in my sight. And it came to pass, when the evil spirit from God was upon Saul, that David took a harp, and played with his

200

hand: so Saul was refreshed, and was well, and the evil spirit departed from him" (1Samuel 16: 14-23 KJV).

A servant's heart is one of the characteristics every believer must have, because our Lord taught and demonstrated it to the disciples, "If I then your Lord and Teacher (Master) have washed your feet, you ought (it is your duty, you are under obligation, you owe it) to wash one another's feet" (John 13:14-15 Amp).

David's character of being a good steward of what his father had entrusted him with made him a person of influence and significant in God's sight. We cannot have our own if we do not know how to take care of others. Secondly, God will not entrust us with much if we are unfaithful with the little.

His character made him a great leader. Our Lord taught his disciples and all His followers. "But this is not to be so among you; instead, whoever desires to be great among you must be your servant. And whoever wishes to be most important and first in rank among you must be slave of all" (Mark 10:43-44, Amp).

David was anointed three times before he became the King of Israel. He was anointed first by Samuel when God rejected King Saul as the King over Israel (1 Samuel 16). Secondly, he was anointed as the King over Judah just after the death of King Saul, "Then the men of Judah came, and they anointed David King over the house of Judah. He was King over only the tribe of Judah then the entire twelve tribes of Israel.

The third anointing was by the elders of Judah after the death of King Saul (2 Samuel 5:3). They saw the greatness and the potential in him. He made a covenant with them at Hebron before the LORD, and they anointed him King over Israel.

He was really proven in his position as a King. He went through a lot of nightmares, but they all came to an end because he knew how to wait on God. Everything that has a beginning has an ending. Only God is eternal; all created things have a beginning and ending. All the troubles, failures and pain you are going through would come to an end someday so hold on to the promises of God.

King David overlooked the wilderness and "dead end" roads he had to go through while he waited expectantly for his reward from God.

We cannot be good stewards if we are not good investors and maintainers like David. Every good steward tries to invest that which has been entrusted to him or her.

A faithful steward works hard and invests much in order to increase. Besides hardworking, a faithful steward will try to maintain the property or the finances of the master. To every Christian reading this book the Lord Jesus is the Master! He expects us to be wise and resourceful.

All living or non-living things need maintenance. Buildings, transportation vehicles, equipment, etc need maintenance. Trees shed their leaves seasonally, and get new leaves during the spring or "rainy season" in some parts of the world Therefore every steward or administrator should be sensitive to the Master's needs, times and season concerning the assignment given to them.

For instance, the Levites were responsible for maintaining the Temple. They did their job diligently. Now every believer has to take care of his/her body which is the temple of the Holy Spirit, then we can all take care of the Church corporately. If you destroy your body God will destroy it. Sexual sins like pornography, fornication, adultery, homosexuality is the main targeted sin that cause people to fall from the grace of God. Our bodies do not belong to us. They belong to God! (1 Corinthians 6:19-20)

Speaking about the body, we cannot be eating junk food, or overeating most of the time and expect to be healthy; it is not going to work. Though the spirit gives life and the body profits nothing, we are responsible for whatever we do to or with our bodies.

In the parable of the king's ten servants in the gospel of Luke (19:11-27) the Lord Jesus tells us how two of them invested and increased the money they had for their master. We all have twenty four hours a day. How profitable do you use your time? Your heart is always where your treasures are.

God has given us gifts so that we would use them to build others up and advance His Kingdom. Moreover these gifts will make room for us and bring us before great men which are notable in King David's story. We have to develop our gifts.

For instance if you have the gift of leadership, you need to know how to set goals, train your followers, employees etc. You have to lead by example.

Probably you may be discouraged now either because of your own faults or someone else's and have stopped going to Church or have vacated the sphere of influence God has called you to. Maybe you are waiting on God but He is rather waiting on you to arise.

We are the stewards of God's resources on earth according to the Scriptures "The heavens are the LORD's heavens, but the earth he has given to the children of man" (Psalms 115:16). God is a KING. Every King wants his Kingdom to dominate. Therefore God wants the knowledge of His glory to cover the earth as the waters cover the seas.

We read the original intent of God from the book of Genesis where God gave Adam dominion over the earth. Unfortunately, the first Adam traded it to the devil for power and earthly wisdom in the Garden of Eden. Fortunately for us, God had already made provision for the Second Adam (Jesus) to come and restore all things to man (Genesis 3:15).

In one of the parables about the Kingdom of God one can relate to why God will applaud the faithful servants with "well-done" (Matthew 25:21, 23). It was because the servant did what the master required of him.

We live in a generation where science, technology and electronics have developed and advanced so much that some of us do not have enough time for the Creator. Some people spend hours on the internet, television, amusements, etc, and ironically have no time to fellowship with the Lord or even to use their gifts and talents.

The only time they have for Him is Sunday during the service time… between one and two hours. We will give account of what we do with our time. That was why the Lord Jesus said we should watch and pray (Matthew 26:41). Definitely, we cannot be praying and watching 24/7, but if we walk in the spirit and are led by the Spirit of God we will not gratify the desires of the flesh, but we will please God in every aspect of our lives. Because we will hear what the Spirit is saying!

Do you want to hear well-done good and faithful servant? The time is short but there is still hope for each of us to be faithful with what God has given us so that He will increase it, and we must strive forward like King David did to hear "well done good and faithful servant (a man or woman) after God's own heart."

God does not waste His resources. The Lord asked the disciples to gather the fragments on both occasions after feeding the multitudes. They were left over but not wasted!

Since God is not a waster, He wants us to be wise as the ant and make use of every opportunity we have. Being good stewards of everything entrusted to us!

Personal Notes.

| |
| |
| |
| |
| |

Chapter 11

Fasting as a lifestyle

Living a self-disciplined Life.

We started our journey through this book with "Humbleness." Now as we approach the topic of fasting, you may realize that King David lived a self-disciplined life through fasting. Actually, his humbleness was partly due to constant fasting, because fasting is a catalyst that helps our prayers to be more effective.

Fasting may sound like a bitter pill to be swallowed, especially in this generation where we have all types of restaurants from different cultures on every corner of the streets.

You probably are also among most of us who have made New Year's resolutions and broken them after a month. Most of us set goals and find ourselves struggling to fulfill them because of lack of self-discipline. But fasting is an important spiritual discipline.

Fasting is rarely mentioned and taught in the Churches here in the U.S. or in most parts of the world these days. However, in Jewish or Muslim communities this is more practiced as part of their beliefs and culture. Some of the Eastern religions like the Buddhist monks also fast (Please note that authentic fasting and prayers must be offered to the true God of Judeo-Christian belief).

Fasting is also practiced during the mourning of the dead in the Jewish tradition. The Hebrew word "afflicted" is normally used to express fasting. The body gets afflicted when we abstain from food and nutrition to sustain itself.

Abstinence of sexual relationships between a husband and wife can also be a discipline of fasting, because the Scripture teaches us to be rejoined to our husbands or wives after a fast, which means to abstain from sexual intimacy during fasting (1 Corinthians 7:5).

However, for some reason people have misinterpreted fasting as abstaining from television, computer, telephone, etc. During biblical times these technologies were not available and even if they were, food and water were the primary sources of fasting.

You can definitely abstain from your addictions to television, telephone and other technologies as a form of fasting if those things are preventing you from having adequate time for God and your family. God has given us wisdom and certainly we have to use it and prioritize our time and life.

The discipline of fasting produces humility. When we fast from food or other things, we deny the flesh of what it wants and as a result our spirits can take control over our flesh.

Since fasting acts as a catalyst, your prayer becomes more powerful and eventually sharpens the individual's spiritual antennae to hear from God. It also sharpens our ability to obey because our weaknesses are exposed when the body is afflicted.

King David was someone who really knew how and when to fast. He wrote in one of his Psalms, "My knees are weak through fasting and my flesh faileth of fatness" (Psalm109:24, KJV). Fasting is self-denial. In one of his Psalms he said God should remember him of his affliction or self-denial (Psalm 132:1),

Fasting draws you closer to God, because you become more vulnerable and humble before God. You will cry out to God for help when your body is feeble and your strength is gone because He is the only One to look to. Even sinners cry out to Him when they are desperate.

The more you fast the more you lose interest in carnal things, unless the fasting is not a true fast. The desires of your heart changes and aligns with that of God's. The desires of the flesh are selfish, greedy, lustful, boastful, etc. All the desires of the flesh are contrary to God's desire for man which are love, joy, peace, etc. (Galatians 5:16-24).

For instance, in the book of Isaiah, we read that the Israelites asked God, "Why have we fasted they say and you do not see it? The facts are that you fast only for strife and debate and to smite with the fist of your wickedness. Fasting as you do today will not cause your voices to be heard on high" (Isaiah 58:3-4, Amp).

God reminded His children who He is, that He is the True and Holy God and we must worship Him in spirit and in truth. He hates injustice. Therefore we cannot pervert justice and expect Him to listen to our hypocritical cry. He wants true humility.

King David had the revelation that he had to decrease, so that God would increase in him. Fasting was a way to that. His lifestyle of fasting was the source of his discipline and his thirst to apprehend and surrender his will and life to God.

Even though David was very successful on the battlefield and in life he remained humble before God. He acknowledged God in almost every circumstance and confessed that God is the source of his strength.

"God is my strength and power. And maketh my way perfect ....
He teacheth my hands to war: so that a bow of steel is broken by
mine arms" (2 Samuel 22:33-35, KJV).

King David was always hungry for more of God. He could not
have enough of Him. He knew that he needed the strength of God
daily. He understood that the flesh is selfish. Therefore, in order
to acquire spiritual blessings or intimacy with God it was
imperative that he brought the flesh under subjection. Those who
are desperately hungry for spiritual food can never be satisfied
with physical food.

David learned how to fast from his infancy. In the Jewish
Tradition a whole day is set apart yearly for the entire nation to
fast. This is the Day of Atonement (Leviticus 18:29). They still
observe it and other ancient festivals. It is a day that the High
Priest goes to the Holy of Holies to atone for the sins of the people
with animal sacrifices.

King David knew the importance of fasting as a Jew. However,
from the Scriptures it's likely he was more devoted to it than the
average Jew. Some of the Jews, especially the Pharisees, did fast
constantly; however it was a prideful discipline to make people
believe that they are more spiritual and holier than others.

Fasting does not make us spiritual if we are missing the main
ingredient of love for God and man. It does not change God but it
changes us. It causes us to yield to God's Spirit and be
transformed into the likeness of God.

The Jews and the early Church are our examples on why and how
to fast because the gospel came from the Jews. The Apostle Paul

wrote in his letter to the early church in Rome: "For I am not ashamed of the gospel of Christ for it is the power of God unto salvation to everyone that believeth; to the Jews first and also to the Greek" (Romans 1:16).

The Scriptures prove that King David fasted for his son in wedlock, when God's judgment was on him through the Prophet Nathan (2 Samuel 12:15:17, 22).

God sent the Prophet Nathan to expose King David's sin at a time David thought his sin of adultery and murder were covered. The child died even though David repented and fasted on his behalf. He loved his child so much that he was willing to do whatever he could to save his life.

How often have you fasted for your children or loved ones when they are struggling in life? Fasting is a time especially for problems like drug addiction, alcoholism, sickness and important decision-making. Fasting helps us to hold on longer when we want to give up quickly.

I encourage you to practice fasting for your loved ones and experience the benefits for yourself. I have heard from a few people including my Apostle, Dr. Che Ahn, who have fasted weekly for their families over several years and now every soul is saved in the household. I have been doing that myself for many years. Though not everyone is saved yet I believe everyone will eventually be saved.

Many of the problems you and your children are experiencing are demonically influenced and it takes only the power of God to break through with prayer and fasting. Since the scripture tells us we wrestle not against flesh and blood, but against the powers, evil forces according to the Scriptures. (Ephesians 6: 10-18). These are very wicked spirits who cause chaos in our families and communities.

It is recorded that David fasted and put on sackcloth when King Saul died. He should have rejoiced over his death because Saul was wicked and he chased David relentlessly, wanting to kill him.

The sackcloth is a cloth that the Jews wear in times of mourning. David mourned and fasted instead of celebration (2 Samuel 1:12).

How many people were like David, who mourned and fasted for his enemy who died? We easily forget at times about our humble beginning; yes, how easy it is for man to forget that it is God who is our strength.

David fasted before and during his reign as a King over Israel and Judah. It was his lifestyle. First of all he was hungry for more of God. Secondly, it became some sort of spiritual exercise for him.

For instance, some of us do some sort of exercise daily to bring our bodies into the right shape. Others are on diets, yoga and so forth (Please note that Yoga is not just an exercise it's a form of worship one of the goddesses fro India, therefore yoga is not for Christians.) When such exercises are turned into the positive way like fasting it would benefit you. People who are on a diet could turn it to be a spiritual exercise by adding prayers to that!

Does King David's disciplined-life speak of you; bringing your body into subjection to the Spirit so that you can live a disciplined life?

His fasting was genuine – he humbled himself before God and for God to bring justice to the oppressed.

Fasting can be practiced for many challenges in our lives. Fasting bring healing. It could be physical healing, mental, financial, or even healing of the land that has been cursed.

Healing through Fasting.

The disciples asked the Lord Jesus privately after He had healed a boy who was suffering from epilepsy, why they could not heal him. His answer was, "This kind can come forth by nothing but by prayer and fasting" (Matthew17:21).

In this passage, Jesus was showing the disciples they were faithless. The intimate relation with the Father through prayer and fasting would increase their faith and power to cast those spirits out.

Please note that at this point Jesus had already sent them to preach, raise the dead, etc (Matthew 10:1-8). Even though this was a physical sickness it had a spiritual connection.

For us to manifest as the sons and daughters of God we really need to make it part of our lifestyle, especially with leaders. Though it is spiritual, it has some other benefits.

We can find many diseases and infirmities have demonic influence. Fasting is especially effective against spiritual attack and is also good for our bodies according to medical science.

Medical Science on Fasting.

Fasting is a healthy way to detox your body. Drinking more water or juice before and during a fast is very beneficial in cleansing all your systems, allowing the body to be rejuvenated, restored and refreshed.

According to research by investigator and Director of Cardiovascular and Genetic Epidemiology, Benjamin D. Horne, fasting causes hunger or stress. In response to it, your body releases more cholesterol and utilizes fat instead of glucose as a source of energy.

This in turn decreases the count of fat cells. And the lesser fat cells a body has, lesser are the chances that it will have diabetes or insulin resistance. The study further concluded that fasting is also helpful in reducing other cardiac risk factors like triglycerides, weight and blood sugar levels.

This expands on a study in 2007 that revealed reduced risks of Coronary Heart Disease linked to fasting. Coronary Heart Disease is one of the main causes of death among men and women in the U.S. The study was presented at the Annual Scientific sessions of American College of Cardiology in New Orleans. Dated May 11. 2011.

Fasting can bring healing to our land when there are draughts and famine. From history one can conclude that God can shut the windows of heaven for various reasons, resulting in drought: Sins, such as bloodshed, idolatry, sexual immorality, pride, corruption in government, or the sins of the people living in a given area. And even sins in the Church can result in God's wrath like drought, famine etc in certain areas or nations.

However, when we truly repent and humble ourselves with fasting God could heal the land, "When I shut up the heavens so that there is no rain, or command locusts to devour the land or send a plague among my people, if my people, who are called by my name, will humble themselves and pray and seek my face and turn from their wicked ways, then I will hear from heaven, and I will forgive their sin and will heal their land"(2 Chronicles 7:13-14).

We can read Scripture references in the book of Joel chapters one and two. The Prophet encouraged the people of Israel that God would bring a restoration to all that have been destroyed as they humble themselves with fasting.

In some US states like Texas and California where severe drought has been experienced for several years, some Christians have worked with politicians to pray and fast for rain and have had positive results.

Pastors, Elders, Deacons, Ministers etc. should be encouraged to participate in fasting and prayer meetings. Sometimes some of us want the congregation to fast while we exempt ourselves. We should lead by example. Like the Prophet Joel, he called the leaders to proclaim a fast and that they should humble themselves in the Temple. That means the congregation would see their brokenness and they would join.

We can conclude from both the New and the Old Testaments that people did fast for various reasons. Some fasted to mourn the death of a loved one or during a national tragedy (Judges 20:26).

An example of a national tragedy was when the tribe of Benjamin (one of the twelve tribes of Israel) attacked and destroyed the Israelites, their own brothers.

They slaughtered eighteen thousand men of war from Israel. Some men from the tribe of Benjamin raped a woman whose husband was in the tribe of Levite. The Levite wanted justice by asking the Benjamites to bring those responsible for justice.

They refused and the rest of the tribes attacked the Bejamintes with the authority from God. They burned down the cities of the Benjamites and killed about twenty five thousand soldiers. The Israelites mourned and fasted on this occasion.

On another account the Israelites fasted as a sign of repentance and pleaded with Samuel who was their Judge and Prophet to intercede on their behalf, because the Ark of the Covenant had been taken away from them. Not only was the Ark taken away from them but they were also harassed and intimidated by the Philistines. Samuel cried out to God and He thundered a great noise on the Philistines and brought them to confusion. They were then smitten by the Israelites and Samuel took a stone, and set it between Mizpeh and Shen, and called it 'Ebenezer "saying thus far has the Lord helped us" (1Samuel 7:12).

In the book of Esther we read how the Israelites were in exile in the land of Susa during the reign of King Xerxes (Persian King). The Israelites fasted three days and nights because Haman, a wicked official at the palace had plotted for Mordecai to be hanged for not bowing down to the him (Esther 3:2).

The offense of one person affected the entire nation. In the book of Joshua we have another example of where one person's sin affected an entire nation. (Please read Joshua chapter 7). But God is always faithful to deliver His people. The entire Jewish community and Mordecai were to be exterminated but Queen

Esther, his adopted orphaned cousin, would help save the Israelites.

As the King's official, Haman was responsible for ordering the extermination of the entire Jewish community, both young and old. Haman exalted himself and wanted people to bow down to him. Mordecai refused to bow and that bred the hatred not only for Mordecai but for all the Jews (Esther 3:5).

Even though God's Name is not mentioned in the book of Esther, the writer makes known God's sovereignty in delivering His people through fasting (Esther 4:1-3, 16; 9:1-4).

The Bible records many of these great men and women of God who fasted. Moses fasted for forty days when he was on Mount Sinai where God gave him the Ten Commandments (Deuteronomy 9:9).

Elijah fasted for forty days and nights after fleeing from Jezebel after destroying the prophets of Baal (1 Kings 18:40).

The Lord Jesus fasted for forty days and nights after being tempted by the devil.

Forty is a significant biblical number which meant "testing."

Although" Forty "days of fasting seems to be commonly recorded in scripture, you should NOT attempt to fast this long without direction from God and also learning how to do a fast safely. Fasting for forty days can be fatal if not done properly.

If God were to direct you to do a lengthy fast He will also strengthen you physically. He will give you the necessary strength you need to protect you from all the attack of the enemy.

It appears that also John the Baptist fasted, even though the scripture does not say it directly. However, Jesus' dialogue with the religious leaders insinuates that he did.

A question arose from the religious leaders to our Lord, "Then John's disciples came and asked Him "How is it that we and the Pharisees fast, but your disciples do not fast?" (Matthew 9:14). This question seems to indicate that he fasted with his disciples.

Ezra, Nehemiah, Daniel, and almost all the faithful men and women used by God fasted for His direction, protection, revelation, understanding, repentance, consecration (setting oneself apart) in impossible situations.

The Apostles also fasted on various occasions.

"While they were worshipping the Lord and fasting, the Holy Spirit said Set apart Barnabas and Saul for the work to which I have called them so after they had fasted and prayed, they placed their hands on them and sent them off" (Acts 13:2-3, NIV).

We also have recorded in the Bible that some people fasted for evil purposes or to kill (1 Kings 21:9-14).

Queen Jezebel proclaimed a fast to murder Naboth, because he would not give his vineyard to her husband king Ahab of Israel for a ransom. In this we see that Satan always imitates or counterfeits whatever God does, instigating his followers to fast in order to destroy the plans and purposes of God.

217

Naboth was from the city of Jezreel, where the royal palace of King Ahab was. Naboth had a vineyard which he inherited from his family. The site of his vineyard was in a strategic position because it was close to King Ahab's palace. The king wanted to buy it or exchanged it for another land, but Naboth refused and Queen Jezebel instructed him to be killed. God punished the entire household of King Ahab because of what his wife did.

Fasting is a sacrifice and must be done with good motives, not to kill, destroy or bring curses on a land, which was the motive of Queen Jezebel and others. Since people from different religions fast, the motive and whom their sacrifice is offered to would determined which fast it is whether it is a true or fake fasting.

The devil can take our inheritance if we are not vigilant. You should never give away your inheritance because it is your legacy to pass on to the next generation.

"A good man leaveth an inheritance for his children's children, and the wealth of the wicked is laid up for the just" (Proverbs 13:22, KJV).

"We are seated with Christ in the heavenly realm" (Ephesians 1:18-20). Christ is our inheritance.

In another passage of the Bible, some Jews plotted to falsely accuse Paul in order to kill him. This was not surprising to Paul, because he was on his way to Jerusalem when he received a prophecy from the Prophet Agabus in Cesarea. The Jews in Jerusalem would tie him and hand him over to be persecuted (Acts 21:7-12).

218

Those people planned to fast till they killed Paul. "And when it was day, certain of the Jews banded together, and bound themselves under a curse, saying that they would not eat nor drink till they had killed Paul" (Acts 23:12, KJV).

Fasting and prayers bring God's redemption plan in your life or the earth into fulfillment. In the gospel of Luke, it is recorded about a devoted woman who prayed and fasted day and night for the redemption of Israel:

"And there was one Anna, a prophetess, the daughter of Phanuel of the tribe of Asher: she was of a great age, and had lived with her husband for seven years from her virginity: and she was a widow of about four score and four years which departed not from the temple, but served God with fasting and prayers night and day" (Luke 2: 36-37).

The Prophets and Kings fasted, Jesus fasted and his disciples later fasted, therefore; this is a spiritual discipline the church should embrace as well.

The Lord taught about Fasting

When you fast, do not look gloomy like the hypocrites, for they neglect their appearance, so that they may appear to others to be fasting. Amen, I say to you, they have received their reward. But when you fast, anoint your head and wash your face, so that you may not appear to be fasting, except to your Father who is hidden. And your Father who sees what is hidden will repay you" (Matthew 6: 16-18).

Fasting must always be accompanied with prayer, if not it

becomes a ritual, a diet or hunger strike. During fasting, the Word of God must be a priority for you; reading, studying, worship and meditating on the Word.

As we abstain from physical food, we strengthen ourselves by increasing our spiritual food, the Word of God.

Fasting and Temptation

The Lord was tempted by the devil after fasting forty days, and He overcame him with the Word of God. "Then Jesus was led up by the Spirit into the wilderness to be tempted by the devil. And when He had fasted forty days and forty nights, afterward He was hungry. Now when the tempter came to Him, he said, 'If You are the Son of God, command that these stones become bread.

But He answered and said, "It is written, 'Man shall not live by bread alone, but by every word that proceeds from the mouth of God" (Matthew 4:1-4).

In my own personal experience I have observed a lot of temptations during and after fasting. The devil comes to distract us during a fast because he knows we are strengthened and he is weakened when we fast. From the Scriptures we read that Satan did not leave the Lord Jesus alone. He tried to tempt Him several times till Satan finally gave up (Matthew 4: 5-11).

The devil's objective is to keep us from fasting because he knows his power will be broken and his works exposed.

Temptation is different from tests or trials. Temptation always leads to seduction, enticing and sin. It is always from the devil. It is a way to cause someone to fall into trouble or disaster. While tests and trials are from God which lead to developing our character through perseverance and eventually result in promotions (James 1:2-4, 13-14).

Demonic forces normally will tempt you with food and whatever excites your flesh. It is not a coincidence that you often would be offered your favorite meal, snack or drink during a fast. No one may know you are fasting, but guess what, the devil knows. Fasting can present many challenges.

Fasting can also affect your body temperature. In recent fasts I have felt really cold like I was in a deep freezer. The lack of food can bring down your body temperature. People who fast regularly can attest to that. Therefore too much of it can cause anemia.

King David certainly went through temptations in times of fasting. The Scriptures say his knees were weak because of fasting. He did not have a car, motor bike or bicycle like you may have. Can you imagine how inconvenient it was?

But he was faithful in the discipline of fasting. He knew the benefits and it made him committed.

Finally, there are different kinds of fasting. Here are some notes on the reasons why we fast.

Why do we fast?

* To humble ourselves; for the flesh to submit and our spirit to take control.

* To get direction and protection from God (Ezra 8:21-23).

* For God to stand on our behalf (Esther 3:1-6, 4:15-17, 2 Chronicles 20:1-4).

* For more spiritual insight and understanding (Daniel 10:1-3).

* For the Kingdom of God to be established (Luke 2:36).

* To set the oppressed free (Isaiah 58:6-10).

* For sins to be covered or forgiven–Day of Atonement (Leviticus 16:29).

* For our ministry to be effective (Luke 4:1-2, Acts 13:2).

* For healing the sick or the land (2 Chronicles 7:14, Matthew.17:21, 2 Samuel 12:15-16).

* For your nation and people in times of desperate situations and when there is a reproach on the people (Nehemiah1:4-5).

Types of Fasting

Complete Fasting- This is a complete abstinence of food and in some cases water. Abstinence of water should be a maximum of three days unless God specifically instructs you otherwise. Under normal circumstances, the average person cannot normally fast longer than three days without water. The body starts to dehydrate after 72 hours. It is therefore dangerous to fast longer than three days. Example of complete fast is Esther and the Jews- Three days without food and water; our Lord's fasting for forty days without food.

Partial Fasting– This is normally called a Daniel fast. It is mainly fruits and vegetables, no meat (beef, pork, fish etc), sugar, or starchy foods.

The duration of the fast should depend on a conviction and revelation from the Holy Spirit. It could be forty days, one, two, or three weeks. It can also be just a couple of hours.

Normally the Jews fast from sunrise to sunset or 6 AM to 6 PM. It is called the Jerusalem fast. It is also partial.

However, some fast a half day, 6 AM to 12 PM, or 6 to 3 PM if you have health issues. You do not take breakfast; when you take it you have already broken the fast. It is assumed that the body fasts at nights while we sleep; so eating in the morning breaks the fast automatically. That is why it is called Breakfast.

Days of Fasting-Some believe it is more effective on Sundays, Wednesdays, and Fridays, because these are the days that the devil normally works effectively. I think the Lord was crucified on Friday, and was raised on Sunday.

And Wednesday being the middle of the week a lot of Churches have their services. And being the mid-week you may need more effort and input to complete the week since tiredness, frustration and retreat may begin to set in.

Maybe that is why some people believe Wednesday is a good day to fast. The founders of the Methodist Church instituted fasting on Wednesdays and Fridays. They would not ordain a minister until they know he can fast on Wednesdays and Fridays from 6 AM till at least 3 PM.

How do we fast?

Usually it is good to find a promise Scripture that relates to your reason for fasting. Also meditate on additional Scripture to help activate your faith. The Holy Spirit will always give you the purpose for your fast. It is also important to make a list of things you are believing God for, during and after the fast. There will certainly be some breakthrough on the list.

It is important to eat very light and drink enough water (at least a half gallon) a few days or a day before your fast (especially a long one). This is needed to start your detoxification process. Also avoid eating too much meat, chicken or fried foods just before you start the fast.

The best recommended foods to eat are fruits and vegetables to prevent constipation. You can drink water, lemon juice and cayenne pepper during a fast which is good for cleansing your system. However, be cautious with lemon because too much acid can be dangerous. Cayenne pepper is very spicy and should also be balanced. I would recommend probably a half gallon of water to less than a half teaspoon full of the pepper with a small size lemon. (Please you may use just a little bit at the beginning so that you don't hurt yourself.

Drinking distilled water is best. However, you can drink any clean water except tap water. Make sure to drink slightly warm water at about room temperature.

Avoid drinking cold water on an empty stomach because it can make you sick. You can also drink juices (but be careful of acidic juices). I recommend drinking sugar-free juices as well as diluting them.

Drinking a little bit of honey with lemon in warm water is also very beneficial for cleansing.

Getting quality time to read and meditate on Scripture is very important. This is vital in helping you not to yield to breaking your fast. Keep your mind on God and His Word because the devil knows when we are vulnerable.

Keep a journal and write down any impressions that come from the Lord throughout the course of the day and during your reading and meditation of Scripture.

If you take vitamins or medications you need to take into consideration the risk involved before you fast. Make sure to ask your doctor if you are healthy enough to handle a fast. When you are taking medication you need to eat before and after taking your medicine. The same goes with vitamins, so it is not advisable to take them on an empty stomach unless it is a partial fast. This can cause headaches and also stimulates your appetite.

It is important to maintain sufficient hours of sleep. Get into the right perspective and mindset during your fast because you are making a sacrifice to God.

King David lost weight from fasting. He was feeble and afflicted in body, soul and mind. He said his knees and strength were weak because of fasting (Psalm 109:24).

Expect to lose weight when you fast, especially during a long fast. The devil will whisper into your ears. Some of the thoughts are, "you will be ugly, you will be skinny, you might get ulcers and people will be laughing at you."

There will be all types of distractions and deceptions. However you will get a break through if you focus on the Lord and do not quit. You will surely make it.

Breaking the Fast!

Breaking the fast is very important because your tendency is to eat everything you get your hands on. Please remember that your intestines have been empty, especially if it is a long fast. They contract during fasting, because they are like elastic. They expand when food gets into the stomach.

Avoid all caffeine products, teas and chocolate at least a day before, during and immediately after the fast, as much as possible.

This can cause headaches and also stimulates your appetite. Chocolate can cause your stomach to be upset. Avoid dehydration by making sure you take plenty of fluid.

After your fast your intestines have been empty for a long time and have contracted. Eating too much too soon may cause constipation and discomfort.

Limit spicy foods after your fast because they can erode the lining of your intestines. You want to make sure you have a full stomach before eating spicy foods.

Avoid drinking acidic juices like orange juice after your fast.

Mild soups, fruits and vegetables are good foods to break your fast with.

If you fast seven or more days, avoid fried and solid foods.

If you have an upset stomach or diarrhea after breaking it, drink a lot of apple juice (100% with no sugar).

Practical Way of Fasting – Making Fasting Easier

If you have never fasted before, start your first fast from 6 AM to noon, then you can do it 6 AM to 3 PM, then 6 AM to 6 PM.

You will soon progress into being a "General" in fasting.

Regular fasting is a way to live a disciplined lifestyle as a believer. If we follow the footsteps of King David, we will learn to bring our flesh under submission so our spirit will commune and receive from God.

"Is this the kind of fast I have chosen, only a day for.." Isaiah 58:6.

Personal Notes.

In conclusion to this book I will say David desired to get closer to God, and he was willing to do whatever it took. David did not seek fame, he just wanted God's Name to be glorified through him God's eyes are running to and fro on the earth, seeking for men and women's hearts that are perfect like King David. God wants to show Himself strong through you and I so the world will know Him. I pray that we will have the heart of King David!

I would like you to pray the prayers below if you do not have a personal relationship with the Lord Jesus Christ, or if you want to rededicate your life to the Lord. The Scripture says you should not harden your heart when you hear God's voice. Maybe you picked this book by chance or out of curiosity. Please know that this wasn't an accident or coincident. God wants you to know that He loves you and does not want you to perish in hell. There is a chance while you are alive to accept His Son Jesus as your Lord and Savior. Come just as you are. Only God is Perfect!

Prayer

"Dear God, I come to you with all my heart. I believe that Jesus Christ died for my sins. I invite you dear Jesus into my heart. Come into my life. I repent of all my sins. Forgive me and cleanse me with your Blood. Fill me with your Holy Spirit and reveal yourself to me in an experiential way so that my life will bring glory to you. In Jesus' Name, Amen!"

Please look for a local Church and be part of it!

Shalom!

Made in the USA
Charleston, SC
18 September 2015